The Giver

and Related Readings

McDougal Littell
A HOUGHTON MIFFLIN COMPANY
Evanston, Illinois   Boston   Dallas

Acknowledgments

American Library Association: "Newbery Award Acceptance Speech" by Lois Lowry, from *Journal of Youth Services in Libraries*, Vol. 7, #4, Summer 1994, Copyright © 1994. Reprinted with permission of the American Library Association.

D'Jimo Kouyate: "The Role of the Griot in West African Society" by D'Jimo Kouyate, from *Talk That Talk*, edited by Linda Goss and Marian E. Barnes. By permission of the author.

Bantam Doubleday Dell Publishing Group, Inc.: "Jeremiah's Song" by Walter Dean Myers, from *Visions* by Donald R. Gallo, Editor. Copyright © 1987 by Walter Dean Myers. Used by permission of Dell Books, a division of Bantam Doubleday Dell Publishing Group, Inc.

Don Congdon Associates, Inc.: "The Pedestrian" by Ray Bradbury, from *The Reporter*, published by Fortnightly Publishing Co. Copyright 1951, renewed © 1979 by Ray Bradbury. Reprinted by permission of Don Congdon Associates, Inc.

Dan Jaffee: "The Forecast" by Dan Jaffee, from *Prairie Schooner*. Copyright © 1964 by Dan Jaffee. By permission of the author.

Bruce Coville: "Old Glory" by Bruce Coville. Copyright © 1991 by Bruce Coville. By permission of the author.

Continued on page 220.

The Giver by Lois Lowry. Copyright © 1993 by Lois Lowry. Reprinted by special arrangement with Houghton Mifflin Company.

Illustration by Ruben Ramos.
Author photo: Copyright © 1987 Amanda Smith.

ISBN 0-395-77529-9

67—DCI—02 01 00 99 98

Contents

Continued

The Giver

Lois Lowry

Chapter 1

It was almost December, and Jonas was beginning to be frightened. No. Wrong word, Jonas thought. Frightened meant that deep, sickening feeling of something terrible about to happen. Frightened was the way he had felt a year ago when an unidentified aircraft had overflown the community twice. He had seen it both times. Squinting toward the sky, he had seen the sleek jet, almost a blur at its high speed, go past, and a second later heard the blast of sound that followed. Then one more time, a moment later, from the opposite direction, the same plane.

At first, he had been only fascinated. He had never seen aircraft so close, for it was against the rules for Pilots to fly over the community. Occasionally, when supplies were delivered by cargo planes to the landing field across the river, the children rode their bicycles to the riverbank and watched, intrigued, the unloading and then the takeoff directed to the west, always away from the community.

But the aircraft a year ago had been different. It was not a squat, fat-bellied cargo plane but a needle-nosed single pilot jet. Jonas, looking around anxiously, had seen others—adults as well as children—stop what they were doing, and wait, confused, for an explanation of the frightening event.

Then all of the citizens had been ordered to go into the nearest building and stay there. IMMEDIATELY, the rasping voice through the speakers had said. LEAVE YOUR BICYCLES WHERE THEY ARE.

Instantly, obediently, Jonas had dropped his bike on its side on the path behind his family's dwelling.

He had run indoors and stayed there, alone. His parents were both at work, and his little sister, Lily, was at the Childcare Center where she spent her after-school hours.

Looking through the front window, he had seen no people: none of the busy afternoon crew of Street Cleaners, Landscape Workers, and Food Delivery people who usually populated the community at that time of day. He saw only the abandoned bikes here and there on their sides; an upturned wheel on one was still revolving slowly.

He had been frightened then. The sense of his own community silent, waiting, had made his stomach churn. He had trembled.

But it had been nothing. Within minutes the speakers had crackled again, and the voice, reassuring now and less urgent, had explained that a Pilot-in-Training had misread his navigational instructions and made a wrong turn. Desperately the Pilot had been trying to make his way back before his error was noticed.

NEEDLESS TO SAY, HE WILL BE RELEASED, the voice had said, followed by silence. There was an ironic tone to that final message, as if the Speaker found it amusing; and Jonas had smiled a little, though he knew what a grim statement it had been. For a contributing citizen to be released from the community was a final decision, a terrible punishment, an overwhelming statement of failure.

Even the children were scolded if they used the term lightly at play, jeering at a teammate who missed a catch or stumbled in a race. Jonas had done it once, had shouted at his best friend, "That's it, Asher! You're released!" when Asher's clumsy error had lost a match for his team. He had been taken aside for a brief and serious talk by the coach, had hung his head with guilt and embarrassment, and apologized to Asher after the game.

Now, thinking about the feeling of fear as he pedaled home along the river path, he remembered that moment of palpable, stomach-sinking terror when the aircraft had streaked above. It was not what he was feeling now with December approaching. He searched for the right word to describe his own feeling.

Jonas was careful about language. Not like his friend, Asher, who talked too fast and mixed things up, scrambling words and phrases until they were barely recognizable and often very funny.

Jonas grinned, remembering the morning that Asher had dashed into the classroom, late as usual, arriving breathlessly in the middle of the chanting of the morning anthem. When the class took their seats at the conclusion of the patriotic hymn, Asher remained standing to make his public apology as was required.

"I apologize for inconveniencing my learning community." Asher ran through the standard apology phrase rapidly, still catching his breath. The Instructor and class waited patiently for his explanation. The students had all been grinning, because they had listened to Asher's explanations so many times before.

"I left home at the correct time but when I was riding along near the hatchery, the crew was separating some salmon. I guess I just got distraught, watching them.

"I apologize to my classmates," Asher concluded. He smoothed his rumpled tunic and sat down.

"We accept your apology, Asher." The class recited the standard response in unison. Many of the students were biting their lips to keep from laughing.

"I accept your apology, Asher," the Instructor said. He was smiling. "And I thank you, because once again you have provided an opportunity for a lesson in language. 'Distraught' is too strong an adjective to describe salmon-viewing." He turned and wrote "distraught" on the instructional board. Beside it he wrote "distracted."

Jonas, nearing his home now, smiled at the recollection. Thinking, still, as he wheeled his bike into its narrow port beside the door, he realized that frightened was the wrong word to describe his feelings, now that December was almost here. It was too strong an adjective.

He had waited a long time for this special December. Now that it was almost upon him, he wasn't frightened, but he was . . . eager, he decided. He was eager for it to come. And he was excited, certainly. All of the Elevens were excited about the event that would be coming so soon.

But there was a little shudder of nervousness when he thought about it, about what might happen.

Apprehensive, Jonas decided. That's what I am.

"Who wants to be the first tonight, for feelings?" Jonas's father asked, at the conclusion of their evening meal.

It was one of the rituals, the evening telling of feelings. Sometimes Jonas and his sister, Lily, argued over turns, over who would get to go first. Their parents, of course, were part of the ritual; they, too, told their feelings each evening. But like all parents—all adults—they didn't fight and wheedle for their turn.

Nor did Jonas, tonight. His feelings were too complicated this evening. He wanted to share them, but he wasn't eager to begin the process of sifting through his own complicated emotions, even with the help that he knew his parents could give.

"You go, Lily," he said, seeing his sister, who was much younger—only a Seven—wiggling with impatience in her chair.

"I felt very angry this afternoon," Lily announced. "My Childcare group was at the play area, and we had a visiting group of Sevens, and they didn't obey the rules at *all*. One of them—a male; I don't know his name—kept going right to the front of the line for the slide, even though the rest of us were all waiting. I felt so angry at him. I made my hand into a fist, like this." She held up a clenched fist and the rest of the family smiled at her small defiant gesture.

"Why do you think the visitors didn't obey the rules?" Mother asked.

Lily considered, and shook her head. "I don't know. They acted like . . . like . . . "

"Animals?" Jonas suggested. He laughed

"That's right," Lily said, laughing too. "Like animals." Neither child knew what the word meant, exactly, but it was often used to describe someone uneducated or clumsy, someone who didn't fit in.

"Where were the visitors from?" Father asked.

Lily frowned, trying to remember. "Our leader told us, when he made the welcome speech, but I can't remember. I guess I wasn't paying attention. It was from another community. They had to leave very early, and they had their midday meal on the bus."

Mother nodded. "Do you think it's possible that their rules may be different? And so they simply didn't know what your play area rules were?"

Lily shrugged, and nodded. "I suppose."

"You've visited other communities, haven't you?" Jonas asked. "My group has, often."

Lily nodded again. "When we were Sixes, we went

and shared a whole school day with a group of Sixes in their community."

"How did you feel when you were there?"

Lily frowned. "I felt strange. Because their methods were different. They were learning usages that my group hadn't learned yet, so we felt stupid."

Father was listening with interest "I'm thinking, Lily," he said, "about the boy who didn't obey the rules today. Do you think it's possible that he felt strange and stupid, being in a new place with rules that he didn't know about?"

Lily pondered that. "Yes," she said, finally.

"I feel a little sorry for him," Jonas said, "even though I don't even know him. I feel sorry for anyone who is in a place where he feels strange and stupid."

"How do you feel now, Lily?" Father asked. "Still angry?"

"I guess not," Lily decided. "I guess I feel a little sorry for him. And sorry I made a fist." She grinned.

Jonas smiled back at his sister. Lily's feelings were always straightforward, fairly simple, usually easy to resolve. He guessed that his own had been, too, when he was a Seven.

He listened politely, though not very attentively, while his father took his turn, describing a feeling of worry that he'd had that day at work: a concern about one of the newchildren who wasn't doing well. Jonas's father's title was Nurturer. He and the other Nurturers were responsible for all the physical and emotional needs of every newchild during its earliest life. It was a very important job, Jonas knew, but it wasn't one that interested him much.

"What gender is it?" Lily asked.

"Male," Father said. "He's a sweet little male with a lovely disposition. But he isn't growing as fast as he should, and he doesn't sleep soundly. We have him in the extra care section for supplementary nurturing, but the committee's beginning to talk about releasing him."

"Oh, *no*," Mother murmured sympathetically. "I know how sad that must make you feel."

Jonas and Lily both nodded sympathetically as well. Release of newchildren was always sad, because they hadn't had a chance to enjoy life within the community yet. And they hadn't done anything wrong.

There were only two occasions of release which were not punishment. Release of the elderly, which was a time of celebration for a life well and fully lived; and release of a newchild, which always brought a sense of what-could-we-have-done. This was especially troubling for the Nurturers, like Father, who felt they had failed somehow. But it happened very rarely.

"Well," Father said, "I'm going to keep trying. I may ask the committee for permission to bring him here at night, if you don't mind. You know what the night-crew Nurturers are like. I think this little guy needs something extra."

"Of course," Mother said, and Jonas and Lily nodded. They had heard Father complain about the night crew before. It was a lesser job, night-crew nurturing, assigned to those who lacked the interest or skills or insight for the more vital jobs of the daytime hours. Most of the people on the night crew had not even been given spouses because they lacked, somehow, the essential capacity to connect to others, which was required for the creation of a family unit.

"Maybe we could even keep him," Lily suggested sweetly, trying to look innocent. The look was fake, Jonas knew; they all knew.

"Lily," Mother reminded her, smiling, "you know the rules."

Two children—one male, one female—to each family unit. It was written very clearly in the rules.

Lily giggled. "Well," she said, "I thought maybe just this once."

Next, Mother, who held a prominent position at the Department of Justice, talked about her feelings. Today a repeat offender had been brought before her, someone who had broken the rules before. Someone who she hoped had been adequately and fairly punished, and who had been restored to his job, his home, his family unit. To see him brought before her a second time caused her overwhelming feelings of frustration and anger. And even guilt that she hadn't made a difference in his life.

"I feel frightened, too, for him," she confessed. "You know that there's no third chance. The rules say that if there's a third transgression, he simply has to be released." Jonas shivered. He knew it happened. There was even a boy in his group of Elevens whose father had been released years before. No one ever mentioned it; the disgrace was unspeakable. It was hard to imagine.

Lily stood up and went to her mother. She stroked her mother's arm.

From his place at the table, Father reached over and took her hand. Jonas reached for the other.

One by one, they comforted her. Soon she smiled, thanked them, and murmured that she felt soothed.

The ritual continued. "Jonas?" Father asked. "You're last, tonight."

Jonas sighed. This evening he almost would have preferred to keep his feelings hidden. But it was, of course, against the rules.

"I'm feeling apprehensive," he confessed, glad that the appropriate descriptive word had finally come to him.

"Why is that, son?" His father looked concerned.

"I know there's really nothing to worry about," Jonas explained, "and that every adult has been through it. I know you have, Father, and you too, Mother. But it's the Ceremony that I'm apprehensive about. It's almost December."

Lily looked up, her eyes wide. "The Ceremony of Twelve," she whispered in an awed voice. Even the smallest children—Lily's age and younger—knew that it lay in the future for each of them.

"I'm glad you told us of your feelings," Father said.

"Lily," Mother said, beckoning to the little girl, "go on now and get into your nightclothes. Father and I are going to stay here and talk to Jonas for a while."

Lily sighed, but obediently she got down from her chair. "Privately?" she asked.

Mother nodded. "Yes," she said, "this talk will be a private one with Jonas."

Chapter 2

Jonas watched as his father poured a fresh cup of coffee. He waited.

"You know," his father finally said, "every December was exciting to me when I was young. And it has been for you and Lily, too, I'm sure. Each December brings such changes."

Jonas nodded. He could remember the Decembers back to when he had become, well, probably a Four. The earlier ones were lost to him. But he observed them each year, and he remembered Lily's earliest Decembers. He remembered when his family received Lily, the day she was named, the day that she had become a One.

The Ceremony for the Ones was always noisy and fun. Each December, all the newchildren born in the previous year turned One. One at a time—there were always fifty in each year's group, if none had been released—they had been brought to the stage by the Nurturers who had cared for them since birth. Some were already walking, wobbly on their unsteady legs, others were no more than a few days old, wrapped in blankets, held by their Nurturers.

"I enjoy the Naming," Jonas said.

His mother agreed, smiling. "The year we got Lily, we knew, of course, that we'd receive our female, because we'd made our application and been approved. But I'd been wondering and wondering what her name would be."

"I could have sneaked a look at the list prior to the ceremony," Father confided. "The committee always makes the list in advance, and it's right there in the office at the Nurturing Center.

"As a matter of fact," he went on, "I feel a little guilty about this. But I *did* go in this afternoon and looked to see if this year's Naming list had been made yet. It was right there in the office, and I looked up number Thirty-six—that's the little guy I've been concerned about—because it occurred to me that it might enhance his nurturing if I could call him by a name. Just privately, of course, when no one else is around."

"Did you find it?" Jonas asked. He was fascinated. It didn't seem a terribly important rule, but the fact that his father had broken a rule at all awed him. He glanced at his mother, the one responsible for adherence to the rules, and was relieved that she was smiling.

His father nodded. "His name—if he makes it to the Naming without being released, of course—is to be Gabriel. So I whisper that to him when I feed him every four hours, and during exercise and playtime. If no one can hear me.

"I call him Gabe, actually," he said, and grinned.

"Gabe." Jonas tried it out. A good name, he decided.

Though Jonas had only become a Five the year that they acquired Lily and learned her name, he remembered the excitement, the conversations at home, wondering about her: how she would look, who she would be, how she would fit into their established family unit. He remembered climbing the steps to the stage with his parents, his father by his side that year instead of with the Nurturers, since it was the year that he would be given a newchild of his own.

He remembered his mother taking the newchild, his sister, into her arms, while the document was read to the assembled family units. "Newchild Twenty-three," the Namer had read. "Lily."

He remembered his father's look of delight, and that his father had whispered, "She's one of my favorites. I was hoping for her to be the one." The crowd had clapped, and Jonas had grinned. He liked his sister's name. Lily, barely awake, had waved her small fist. Then they had stepped down to make room for the next family unit.

"When I was an Eleven," his father said now, "as you are, Jonas, I was very impatient, waiting for the Ceremony of Twelve. It's a long two days. I remember that I enjoyed the Ones, as I always do, but that I didn't pay much attention to the other ceremonies, except for my sister's. She became a Nine that year, and got her bicycle. I'd been teaching her to ride mine, even though technically I wasn't supposed to."

Jonas laughed. It was one of the few rules that was not taken very seriously and was almost *always* broken. The children all received their bicycles at Nine; they were not allowed to ride bicycles before then. But almost always, the older brothers and sisters had secretly taught the younger ones. Jonas had been thinking already about teaching Lily.

There was talk about changing the rule and giving the bicycles at an earlier age. A committee was studying the idea. When something went to a committee for study, the people always joked about it. They said that the committee members would become Elders by the time the rule change was made.

Rules were very hard to change. Sometimes, if it was a very important rule—unlike the one governing the age for bicycles—it would have to go, eventually, to The Receiver for a decision. The Receiver was the most important Elder. Jonas had never even seen him, that he knew of; someone in a position of such importance lived and worked alone. But the committee would never bother The Receiver with a question about bicycles; they would simply fret and argue about it themselves for years, until the citizens forgot that it had ever gone to them for study.

His father continued. "So I watched and cheered when my sister, Katya, became a Nine and removed her hair ribbons and got her bicycle," Father went on. "Then I didn't pay much attention to the Tens and Elevens. And *finally*, at the end of the second day, which seemed to go on forever, it was my turn. It was the Ceremony of Twelve."

Jonas shivered. He pictured his father, who must have been a shy and quiet boy, for he was a shy and quiet man, seated with his group, waiting to be called to the stage. The Ceremony of Twelve was the last of the Ceremonies. The most important.

"I remember how proud my parents looked—and my sister, too; even though she wanted to be out riding the bicycle publicly, she stopped fidgeting and was very still and attentive when my turn came.

"But to be honest, Jonas," his father said, "for me there was not the element of suspense that there is with your Ceremony. Because I was already fairly certain of what my Assignment was to be."

Jonas was surprised. There was no way, really, to know in advance. It was a secret selection, made by the leaders of the community, the Committee of Elders, who took the responsibility so seriously that there were never even any jokes made about Assignments.

His mother seemed surprised, too. "How could you have known?" she asked.

His father smiled his gentle smile. "Well, it was clear to me—and my parents later confessed that it had been obvious to them, too—what my aptitude was. I had always loved the newchildren more than anything. When my friends in my age group were holding bicycle races or building toy vehicles or bridges with their construction sets or—"

"All the things I do with my friends," Jonas pointed out, and his mother nodded in agreement.

"I always participated, of course, because as children we must experience all of those things. And I studied hard in school, as you do, Jonas. But again and again, during free time, I found myself drawn to the newchildren. I spent almost all of my volunteer hours helping in the Nurturing Center. Of course the Elders knew that from their observation."

Jonas nodded. During the past year he had been aware of the increasing level of observation. In school, at recreation time, and during volunteer hours, he had noticed the Elders watching him and the other Elevens. He had seen them taking notes. He knew, too, that the Elders were meeting for long hours with all of the instructors that he and the other Elevens had had during their years of school.

"So I expected it, and I was pleased, but not at all surprised, when my Assignment was announced as Nurturer," Father explained.

"Did everyone applaud, even though they weren't surprised?" Jonas asked.

"Oh, of course. They were happy for me, that my Assignment was what I wanted most. I felt very fortunate." His father smiled.

"Were any of the Elevens disappointed, your year?" Jonas asked. Unlike his father, he had no idea what his Assignment would be. But he knew that some would disappoint him. Though he respected his father's work, Nurturer would not be his wish. And he didn't envy Laborers at all.

His father thought. "No, I don't think so. Of course the Elders are so careful in their observations and selections."

"I think it's probably the most important job in our community," his mother commented.

"My friend Yoshiko was surprised by her selection as Doctor," Father said, "but she was thrilled. And let's see, there was Andrei—I remember that when we were boys he never wanted to do physical things. He spent all the recreation time he could with his construction set, and his volunteer hours were always on building sites. The Elders knew that, of course. Andrei was given the Assignment of Engineer and he was delighted."

"Andrei later designed the bridge that crosses the river to the west of town," Jonas's mother said. "It wasn't there when we were children."

"There are rarely disappointments, Jonas. I don't think you need to worry about that," his father reassured him. "And if there are, you know there's an appeal process." But they all laughed at that—an appeal went to a committee for study.

"I worry a little about Asher's Assignment," Jonas confessed. "Asher's such *fun*. But he doesn't really have any serious interests. He makes a game out of everything."

His father chuckled. "You know," he said, "I remember when Asher was a newchild at the Nurturing Center, before he was named. He never cried. He giggled and laughed at everything. All of us on the staff enjoyed nurturing Asher."

"The Elders know Asher," his mother said. "They'll find exactly the right Assignment for him. I don't think you need to worry about him. But, Jonas, let me warn you about something that may not have occurred to you. I know I didn't think about it until after my Ceremony of Twelve."

"What's that?"

"Well, it's the last of the Ceremonies, as you know. After Twelve, age isn't important. Most of us even lose track of how old we are as time passes, though the information is in the Hall of Open Records, and we could go and look it up if we wanted to. What's important is the preparation for adult life, and the training you'll receive in your Assignment."

"I know that," Jonas said. "Everyone knows that."

"But it means," his mother went on, "that you'll move into a new group. And each of your friends will. You'll no longer be spending your time with your group of Elevens. After the Ceremony of Twelve, you'll be with your Assignment group, with those in training. No more volunteer hours. No more recreation hours. So your friends will no longer be as close."

Jonas shook his head. "Asher and I will always be friends," he said firmly. "And there will still be school."

"That's true," his father agreed. "But what your mother said is true as well. There will be changes."

"*Good* changes, though," his mother pointed out. "After my Ceremony of Twelve, I missed my childhood recreation. But when I entered my training for Law and Justice, I found myself with people who shared my interests. I made friends on a new level, friends of all ages."

"Did you still play at all, after Twelve?" Jonas asked.

"Occasionally," his mother replied. "But it didn't seem as important to me."

"I did," his father said, laughing. "I still do. Every day, at the Nurturing Center, I play bounce-on-the-knee, and peek-a-boo, and hug-the-teddy." He reached over and stroked Jonas's neatly trimmed hair. "Fun doesn't end when you become Twelve."

Lily appeared, wearing her nightclothes, in the doorway. She gave an impatient sigh. "This is certainly a very *long* private conversation," she said. "And there are certain people waiting for their comfort object."

"Lily," her mother said fondly, "you're very close to being an Eight, and when you're an Eight, your comfort object will be taken away. It will be recycled to the younger children. You should be starting to go off to sleep without it."

But her father had already gone to the shelf and taken down the stuffed elephant which was kept there. Many of the comfort objects, like Lily's, were soft, stuffed, imaginary creatures. Jonas's had been called a bear.

"Here you are, Lily-billy," he said. "I'll come help you remove your hair ribbons."

Jonas and his mother rolled their eyes, yet they watched affectionately as Lily and her father headed to her sleeping-room with the stuffed elephant that had been given to her as her comfort object when she was born. His mother moved to her big desk and opened her briefcase; her work never seemed to end, even when she was at home in the evening. Jonas went to his own desk and began to sort through his school papers for the evening's assignment. But his mind was still on December and the coming Ceremony.

Though he had been reassured by the talk with his parents, he hadn't the slightest idea what Assignment the Elders would be selecting for his future, or how he might feel about it when the day came.

Chapter 3

"Oh, look!" Lily squealed in delight. "Isn't he cute? Look how tiny he is! And he has funny eyes like yours, Jonas!" Jonas glared at her. He didn't like it that she had mentioned his eyes. He waited for his father to chastise Lily. But Father was busy unstrapping the carrying basket from the back of his bicycle. Jonas walked over to look.

It was the first thing Jonas noticed as he looked at the newchild peering up curiously from the basket. The pale eyes.

Almost every citizen in the community had dark eyes. His parents did, and Lily did, and so did all of his group members and friends. But there were a few exceptions: Jonas himself, and a female Five who he had noticed had the different, lighter eyes. No one mentioned such things; it was not a rule, but was considered rude to call attention to things that were unsettling or different about individuals. Lily, he decided, would have to learn that soon, or she would be called in for chastisement because of her insensitive chatter.

Father put his bike into its port. Then he picked up the basket and carried it into the house. Lily followed behind, but she glanced back over her shoulder at Jonas and teased, "Maybe he had the same Birthmother as you."

Jonas shrugged. He followed them inside. But he had been startled by the newchild's eyes. Mirrors were rare in the community; they weren't forbidden, but there was no real need of them, and Jonas had simply never bothered to look at himself very often even when he found himself in a location where a mirror existed. Now, seeing the newchild and its expression, he was reminded that the light eyes were not only a rarity but gave the one who had them a certain look—what was it? *Depth,* he decided; as if one were looking into the clear water of the river, down to the bottom, where things might lurk which hadn't been discovered yet. He felt self-conscious, realizing that he, too, had that look.

He went to his desk, pretending not to be interested in the newchild. On the other side of the room, Mother and Lily were bending over to watch as Father unwrapped its blanket.

"What's his comfort object called?" Lily asked, picking up the stuffed creature which had been placed beside the newchild in his basket.

Father glanced at it "Hippo," he said.

Lily giggled at the strange word. "Hippo," she repeated, and put the comfort object down again. She peered at the unwrapped newchild, who waved his arms.

"I think newchildren are so cute," Lily sighed. "I hope I get assigned to be a Birthmother."

"Lily!" Mother spoke very sharply. "Don't say that. There's very little honor in that Assignment."

"But I was talking to Natasha. You know the Ten who lives around the corner? She does some of her volunteer hours at the Birthing Center. And she told me that the Birthmothers get wonderful food, and they have very gentle exercise periods, and most of the time they just play games and amuse themselves while they're waiting. I think I'd like that," Lily said petulantly.

"Three years," Mother told her firmly. "Three births, and that's all. After that they are Laborers for the rest of their adult lives, until the day that they enter the House of the Old. Is that what you want, Lily? Three lazy years, and then hard physical labor until you are old?"

"Well, no, I guess not," Lily acknowledged reluctantly.

Father turned the newchild onto his tummy in the basket. He sat beside it and rubbed its small back with a rhythmic motion. "Anyway, Lily-billy," he said affectionately, "the Birthmothers never even get to see newchildren. If you enjoy the little ones so much, you should hope for an Assignment as Nurturer."

"When you're an Eight and start your volunteer hours, you can try some at the Nurturing Center," Mother suggested.

"Yes, I think I will," Lily said. She knelt beside the basket. "What did you say his name is? Gabriel? Hello, Gabriel," she said in a singsong voice. Then she giggled. "Ooops," she whispered. "I believe he's asleep. I guess I'd better be quiet."

Jonas turned to the school assignments on his desk. Some chance of *that,* he thought. Lily was *never* quiet. Probably she should hope for an Assignment as Speaker, so that she could sit in the office with the microphone all day, making announcements. He laughed silently to himself, picturing his sister droning on in the self-important voice that all the Speakers seemed to develop, saying things like, ATTENTION. THIS IS A REMINDER TO FEMALES UNDER NINE THAT HAIR RIBBONS ARE TO BE NEATLY TIED AT ALL TIMES.

He turned toward Lily and noticed to his satisfaction that her ribbons were, as usual, undone and dangling. There would be an announcement like that quite soon, he felt certain, and it would be directed mainly at Lily, though her name, of course, would not be mentioned. Everyone would know.

Everyone had known, he remembered with humiliation, that the announcement ATTENTION. THIS IS A REMINDER TO MALE ELEVENS THAT OBJECTS ARE NOT TO BE REMOVED FROM THE RECREATION AREA AND THAT SNACKS ARE TO BE EATEN, NOT HOARDED had been specifically directed at him, the day last month that he had taken an apple home. No one had mentioned it, not even his parents, because the public announcement had been sufficient to produce the appropriate remorse. He had, of course, disposed of the apple and made his apology to the Recreation Director the next morning, before school.

Jonas thought again about that incident. He was still bewildered by it. Not by the announcement or the necessary apology; those were standard procedures, and he had deserved them—but by the incident itself. He probably should have brought up his feeling of bewilderment that very evening when the family unit had shared their feelings of the day. But he had not been able to sort out and put words to the source of his confusion, so he had let it pass.

It had happened during the recreation period, when he had been playing with Asher. Jonas had casually picked up an apple from the basket where the snacks were kept, and had thrown it to his friend. Asher had thrown it back, and they had begun a simple game of catch.

There had been nothing special about it; it was an activity that he had performed countless times: throw, catch; throw catch. It was effortless for Jonas, and even boring, though Asher enjoyed it, and playing catch was a required activity for Asher because it would improve his hand-eye coordination, which was not up to standards.

But suddenly Jonas had noticed, following the path of the apple through the air with his eyes, that the piece of fruit had—well, this was the part that he couldn't adequately understand—the apple had *changed*. Just for an instant. It had changed in midair, he remembered. Then it was in his hand, and he looked at it carefully, but it was the same apple. Unchanged. The same size and shape: a perfect sphere. The same nondescript shade, about the same shade as his own tunic.

There was absolutely nothing remarkable about the apple. He had tossed it back and forth between his hands a few times, then thrown it again to Asher. And again in the air, for an instant only—it had changed.

It had happened four times. Jonas had blinked, looked around, and then tested his eyesight, squinting at the small print on the identification badge attached to his tunic. He read his name quite clearly. He could also clearly see Asher at the other end of the throwing area. And he had had no problem catching the apple.

Jonas had been completely mystified.

"Ash?" he had called. "Does anything seem strange to you? About the apple?"

"Yes," Asher called back, laughing. "It jumps out of my hand onto the ground!" Asher had just dropped it once again.

So Jonas laughed too, and with his laughter tried to ignore his uneasy conviction that *something* had happened. But he had taken the apple home, against the recreation area rules. That evening, before his parents and Lily arrived at the dwelling, he had held it in his hands and looked at it carefully. It was slightly bruised now, because Asher had dropped it several times. But there was nothing at all unusual about the apple.

He had held a magnifying glass to it. He had tossed it several times across the room, watching, and then rolled it around and around on his desktop, waiting for the thing to happen again.

But it hadn't. The only thing that happened was the announcement later that evening over the speaker, the announcement that had singled him out without using his name, that had caused both of his parents to glance meaningfully at his desk where the apple still lay.

Now, sitting at his desk, staring at his schoolwork as his family hovered over the newchild in its basket, he shook his head, trying to forget the odd incident. He forced himself to arrange his papers and try to study a little before the evening meal. The newchild, Gabriel, stirred and whimpered, and Father spoke softly to Lily, explaining the feeding procedure as he opened the container that held the formula and equipment.

The evening proceeded as all evenings did in the family unit, in the dwelling, in the community: quiet, reflective, a time for renewal and preparation for the day to come. It was different only in the addition to it of the newchild with his pale, solemn, knowing eyes.

Chapter 4

Jonas rode at a leisurely pace, glancing at the bikeports beside the buildings to see if he could spot Asher's. He didn't often do his volunteer hours with his friend because Asher frequently fooled around and made serious work a little difficult. But now, with Twelve coming so soon and the volunteer hours ending, it didn't seem to matter.

The freedom to choose where to spend those hours had always seemed a wonderful luxury to Jonas; other hours of the day were so carefully regulated.

He remembered when he had become an Eight, as Lily would do shortly, and had been faced with that freedom of choice. The Eights always set out on their first volunteer hour a little nervously, giggling and staying in groups of friends. They almost invariably did their hours on Recreation Duty first, helping with the younger ones in a place where they still felt comfortable. But with guidance, as they developed self-confidence and maturity, they moved on to other jobs, gravitating toward those that would suit their own interests and skills.

A male Eleven named Benjamin had done his entire nearly-Four years in the Rehabilitation Center, working with citizens who had been injured. It was rumored that he was as skilled now as the Rehabilitation Directors themselves, and that he had even developed some machines and methods to hasten rehabilitation. There was no doubt that Benjamin would receive his Assignment to that field and would probably be permitted to bypass most of the training.

Jonas was impressed by the things Benjamin had achieved. He knew him, of course, since they had always been groupmates, but they had never talked about the boy's accomplishments because such a conversation would have been awkward for Benjamin. There was never any comfortable way to mention or discuss one's successes without breaking the rule against bragging, even if one didn't mean to. It was a minor rule, rather like rudeness, punishable only by gentle chastisement. But still. Better to steer clear of an occasion governed by a rule which would be so easy to break.

The area of dwellings behind him, Jonas rode past the community structures, hoping to spot Asher's bicycle parked beside one of the small factories or office buildings. He passed the Childcare Center where Lily stayed after school, and the play areas surrounding it. He rode through the Central Plaza and the large Auditorium where public meetings were held.

Jonas slowed and looked at the nametags on the bicycles lined up outside the Nurturing Center. Then he checked those outside Food Distribution; it was always fun to help with the deliveries, and he hoped he would find his friend there so that they could go together on the daily rounds, carrying the cartons of supplies into the dwellings of the community. But he finally found Asher's bicycle—leaning, as usual, instead of upright in its port, as it should have been—at the House of the Old.

There was only one other child's bicycle there, that of a female Eleven named Fiona. Jonas liked Fiona. She was a good student, quiet and polite, but she had a sense of fun as well, and it didn't surprise him that she was working with Asher today. He parked his bicycle neatly in the port beside theirs and entered the building.

"Hello, Jonas," the attendant at the front desk said. She handed him the sign-up sheet and stamped her own official seal beside his signature. All of his volunteer hours would be carefully tabulated at the Hall of Open Records. Once, long ago, it was whispered among the children, an Eleven had arrived at the Ceremony of Twelve only to hear a public announcement that he had not completed the required number of volunteer hours and would not, therefore, be given his Assignment. He had been permitted an additional month in which to complete the hours, and then given his Assignment privately, with no applause, no celebration; a disgrace that had clouded his entire future.

"It's good to have some volunteers here today," the attendant told him. "We celebrated a release this morning, and that always throws the schedule off a little, so things get backed up." She looked at a printed sheet. "Let's see. Asher and Fiona are helping in the bathing room. Why don't you join them there? You know where it is, don't you?"

Jonas nodded, thanked her, and walked down the long hallway. He glanced into the rooms on either side. The Old were sitting quietly, some visiting and talking with one another, others doing handwork and simple crafts. A few were asleep. Each room was comfortably furnished, the floors covered with thick carpeting. It was a serene and slow-paced place, unlike the busy centers of manufacture and distribution where the daily work of the community occurred.

Jonas was glad that he had, over the years, chosen to do his hours in a variety of places so that he could experience the differences. He realized, though, that not focusing on one area meant he was left with not the slightest idea—not even a *guess*—of what his Assignment would be.

He laughed softly. Thinking about the Ceremony again, Jonas? he teased himself. But he suspected that with the date so near, probably all of his friends were, too.

He passed a Caretaker walking slowly with one of the Old in the hall. "Hello, Jonas," the young uniformed man said, smiling pleasantly. The woman beside him, whose arm he held, was hunched over as she shuffled along in her slippers. She looked toward Jonas and smiled, but her dark eyes were clouded and blank. He realized she was blind.

He entered the bathing room with its warm moist air and scent of cleansing lotions. He removed his tunic, hung it carefully on a wall hook, and put on the volunteer's smock that was folded on a shelf.

"Hi, Jonas!" Asher called from the corner where he was kneeling beside a tub. Jonas saw Fiona nearby, at a different tub. She looked up and smiled at him, but she was busy, gently washing a man who lay in the warm water.

Jonas greeted them and the caretaking attendants at work nearby. Then he went to the row of padded lounging chairs where others of the Old were waiting. He had worked here before; he knew what to do.

"Your turn, Larissa," he said, reading the nametag on the woman's robe. "I'll just start the water and then help you up." He pressed the button on a nearby empty tub and watched as the warm water flowed in through the many small openings on the sides. The tub would be filled in a minute and the water flow would stop automatically.

He helped the woman from the chair, led her to the tub, removed her robe, and steadied her with his hand on her arm as she stepped in and lowered herself. She leaned back and sighed with pleasure, her head on a soft cushioned headrest.

"Comfortable?" he asked, and she nodded, her eyes closed. Jonas squeezed cleansing lotion onto the clean sponge at the edge of the tub and began to wash her frail body.

Last night he had watched as his father bathed the newchild. This was much the same: the fragile skin, the soothing water, the gentle motion of his hand, slippery with soap. The relaxed, peaceful smile on the woman's face reminded him of Gabriel being bathed.

And the nakedness, too. It was against the rules for children or adults to look at another's nakedness; but the rule did not apply to newchildren or the Old. Jonas was glad. It was a nuisance to keep oneself covered while changing for games, and the required apology if one had by mistake glimpsed another's body was always awkward. He couldn't see why it was necessary. He liked the feeling of safety here in this warm and quiet room; he liked the expression of trust on the woman's face as she lay in the water unprotected, exposed, and free.

From the corner of his eye he could see his friend Fiona help the old man from the tub and tenderly pat his thin, naked body dry with an absorbent cloth. She helped him into his robe.

Jonas thought Larissa had drifted into sleep, as the Old often did, and he was careful to keep his motions steady and gentle so he wouldn't wake her. He was surprised when she spoke, her eyes still closed.

"This morning we celebrated the release of Roberto," she told him. "It was wonderful."

"I knew Roberto!" Jonas said. "I helped with his feeding the last time I was here, just a few weeks ago. He was a very interesting man."

Larissa opened her eyes happily. "They told his

whole life before they released him," she said. "They always do. But to be honest," she whispered with a mischievous look, "some of the tellings are a little boring. I've even seen some of the Old fall asleep during tellings—when they released Edna recently. Did you know Edna?"

Jonas shook his head. He couldn't recall anyone named Edna.

"Well, they tried to make her life sound meaningful. And of course," she added primly, "all lives *are* meaningful, I don't mean that they aren't. But *Edna*. My goodness. She was a Birthmother, and then she worked in Food Production for years, until she came here. She never even had a family unit."

Larissa lifted her head and looked around to make sure no one was listening. Then she confided, "I don't think Edna was very smart."

Jonas laughed. He rinsed her left arm, laid it back into the water, and began to wash her feet. She murmured with pleasure as he massaged her feet with the sponge.

"But Roberto's life was wonderful," Larissa went on, after a moment. "He had been an Instructor of Elevens—you know how important that is—and he'd been on the Planning Committee. And—goodness, I don't know how he found the time—he also raised two very successful children, and he was *also* the one who did the landscaping design for the Central Plaza. He didn't do the actual labor, of course."

"Now your back. Lean forward and I'll help you sit up." Jonas put his arm around her and supported her as she sat. He squeezed the sponge against her back and began to rub her sharp-boned shoulders. "Tell me about the celebration."

"Well, there was the telling of his life. That is always first. Then the toast. We all raised our glasses and cheered. We chanted the anthem. He made a lovely speech. And several of us made little speeches wishing him well. I didn't, though. I've never been fond of public speaking.

"He was thrilled. You should have seen the look on his face when they let him go."

Jonas slowed the strokes of his hand on her back thoughtfully. "Larissa," he asked, "what happens when they make the actual release? Where exactly did Roberto go?"

She lifted her bare wet shoulders in a small shrug. "I don't know. I don't think anybody does, except the committee. He just bowed to all of us and then walked, like they all do, through the special door in the Releasing Room. But you should have seen his look. Pure happiness, I'd call it."

Jonas grinned. "I wish I'd been there to see it."

Larissa frowned. "I don't know why they don't let children come. Not enough room, I guess. They should enlarge the Releasing Room."

"We'll have to suggest that to the committee. Maybe they'd study it," Jonas said slyly, and Larissa chortled with laughter.

"*Right!*" she hooted, and Jonas helped her from the tub.

Chapter 5

Usually, at the morning ritual when the family members told their dreams, Jonas didn't contribute much. He rarely dreamed. Sometimes he awoke with a feeling of fragments afloat in his sleep, but he couldn't seem to grasp them and put them together into something worthy of telling at the ritual.

But this morning was different. He had dreamed very vividly the night before.

His mind wandered while Lily, as usual, recounted a lengthy dream, this one a frightening one in which she had, against the rules, been riding her mother's bicycle and been caught by the Security Guards.

They all listened carefully and discussed with Lily the warning that the dream had given.

"Thank you for your dream, Lily." Jonas said the standard phrase automatically, and tried to pay better attention while his mother told of a dream fragment, a disquieting scene where she had been chastised for a rule infraction she didn't understand. Together they agreed that it probably resulted from her feelings when she had reluctantly dealt punishment to the citizen who had broken the major rules a second time.

Father said that he had had no dreams.

"Gabe?" Father asked, looking down at the basket where the newchild lay gurgling after his feeding, ready to be taken back to the Nurturing Center for the day.

They all laughed. Dream-telling began with the Threes. If newchildren dreamed, no one knew.

"Jonas?" Mother asked. They always asked,

though they knew how rarely Jonas had a dream to tell.

"I *did* dream last night," Jonas told them. He shifted in his chair, frowning.

"Good," Father said. "Tell us."

"The details aren't clear, really," Jonas explained, trying to recreate the odd dream in his mind "I think I was in the bathing room at the House of the Old."

"That's where you were yesterday," Father pointed out.

Jonas nodded. "But it wasn't really the same. There was a tub, in the dream. But only one. And the real bathing room has rows and rows of them. But the room in the dream was warm and damp. And I had taken off my tunic, but hadn't put on the smock, so my chest was bare. I was perspiring, because it was so warm. And Fiona was there, the way she was yesterday."

"Asher, too?" Mother asked.

Jonas shook his head. "No. It was only me and Fiona, alone in the room, standing beside the tub. She was laughing. But I wasn't. I was almost a little angry at her, in the dream, because she wasn't taking me seriously."

"Seriously about what?" Lily asked.

Jonas looked at his plate. For some reason that he didn't understand, he felt slightly embarrassed. "I think I was trying to convince her that she should get into the tub of water."

He paused. He knew he had to tell it all, that it was not only all right but necessary to tell *all* of a dream. So he forced himself to relate the part that made him uneasy.

"I wanted her to take off her clothes and get into the tub," he explained quickly. "I wanted to bathe her. I had the sponge in my hand. But she wouldn't.

She kept laughing and saying no."

He looked up at his parents. "That's all," he said.

"Can you describe the strongest feeling in your dream, son?" Father asked.

Jonas thought about it. The details were murky and vague. But the feelings were clear, and flooded him again now as he thought. "The *wanting*," he said. "I knew that she wouldn't. And I think I knew that she *shouldn't*. But I wanted it so terribly. I could feel the wanting all through me."

"Thank you for your dream, Jonas," Mother said after a moment. She glanced at Father.

"Lily," Father said, "it's time to leave for school. Would you walk beside me this morning and keep an eye on the newchild's basket? We want to be certain he doesn't wiggle himself loose."

Jonas began to rise to collect his schoolbooks. He thought it surprising that they hadn't talked about his dream at length before the thank you. Perhaps they found it as confusing as he had.

"Wait, Jonas," Mother said gently. "I'll write an apology to your instructor so that you won't have to speak one for being late."

He sank back down into his chair, puzzled. He waved to Father and Lily as they left the dwelling, carrying Gabe in his basket. He watched while Mother tidied the remains of the morning meal and placed the tray by the front door for the Collection Crew.

Finally she sat down beside him at the table. "Jonas," she said with a smile, "the feeling you described as the wanting? It was your first Stirrings. Father and I have been expecting it to happen to you. It happens to everyone. It happened to Father when he was your age. And it happened to me. It will happen someday to Lily.

"And very often," Mother added, "it begins with a dream."

Stirrings. He had heard the word before. He remembered that there was a reference to the Stirrings in the Book of Rules, though he didn't remember what it said. And now and then the Speaker mentioned it. ATTENTION. A REMINDER THAT STIRRINGS MUST BE REPORTED IN ORDER FOR TREATMENT TO TAKE PLACE.

He had always ignored that announcement because he didn't understand it and it had never seemed to apply to him in any way. He ignored, as most citizens did, many of the commands and reminders read by the Speaker.

"Do I have to report it?" he asked his mother.

She laughed. "You did, in the dream-telling. That's enough."

"But what about the treatment? The Speaker says that treatment must take place." Jonas felt miserable. Just when the Ceremony was about to happen, his Ceremony of Twelve, would he have to go away someplace for treatment? Just because of a stupid dream?

But his mother laughed again in a reassuring, affectionate way. "No, no," she said. "It's just the pills. You're ready for the pills, that's all. That's the treatment for Stirrings."

Jonas brightened. He knew about the pills. His parents both took them each morning. And some of his friends did, he knew. Once he had been heading off to school with Asher, both of them on their bikes, when Asher's father had called from their dwelling doorway, "You forgot your pill, Asher!" Asher had groaned good-naturedly, turned his bike, and ridden back while Jonas waited.

It was the sort of thing one didn't ask a friend

about because it might have fallen into that uncomfortable category of "being different." Asher took a pill each morning; Jonas did not. Always better, less rude, to talk about things that were the same.

Now he swallowed the small pill that his mother handed him.

"That's all?" he asked.

"That's all," she replied, returning the bottle to the cupboard. "But you mustn't forget. I'll remind you for the first weeks, but then you must do it on your own. If you forget, the Stirrings will come back. The dreams of the Stirrings will come back. Sometimes the dosage must be adjusted."

"Asher takes them," Jonas confided.

His mother nodded, unsurprised. "Many of your groupmates probably do. The males, at least. And they all will, soon. Females too."

"How long will I have to take them?"

"Until you enter the House of the Old," she explained. "All of your adult life. But it becomes routine; after a while you won't even pay much attention to it."

She looked at her watch. "If you leave right now, you won't even be late for school. Hurry along.

"And thank you again, Jonas," she added, as he went to the door, "for your dream."

Pedaling rapidly down the path, Jonas felt oddly proud to have joined those who took the pills. For a moment, though, he remembered the dream again. The dream had felt pleasurable. Though the feelings were confused, he thought that he had liked the feelings that his mother had called Stirrings. He remembered that upon waking, he had wanted to feel the Stirrings again.

Then, in the same way that his own dwelling

slipped away behind him as he rounded a corner on his bicycle, the dream slipped away from his thoughts. Very briefly, a little guiltily, he tried to grasp it back. But the feelings had disappeared. The Stirrings were gone.

Chapter 6

"Lily, *please* hold still," Mother said again.

Lily, standing in front of her, fidgeted impatiently. "I can tie them myself," she complained. "I always have."

"I know that," Mother replied, straightening the hair ribbons on the little girl's braids. "But I also know that they constantly come loose and more often than not, they're dangling down your back by afternoon. Today, at least, we want them to be neatly tied and to *stay* neatly tied."

"I don't like hair ribbons. I'm glad I only have to wear them one more year," Lily said irritably. "Next year I get my bicycle, too," she added more cheerfully.

"There are good things each year," Jonas reminded her. "This year you get to start your volunteer hours. And remember last year, when you became a Seven, you were so happy to get your front-buttoned jacket?"

The little girl nodded and looked down at herself, at the jacket with its row of large buttons that designated her as a Seven. Fours, Fives, and Sixes all wore jackets that fastened down the back so that they would have to help each other dress and would learn interdependence.

The front-buttoned jacket was the first sign of independence, the first very visible symbol of growing up. The bicycle, at Nine, would be the powerful emblem of moving gradually out into the community, away from the protective family unit.

Lily grinned and wriggled away from her mother.

"And this year you get your Assignment," she said to Jonas in an excited voice. "I hope you get Pilot. And that you take me flying!"

"Sure I will," said Jonas. "And I'll get a special little parachute that just fits you, and I'll take you up to, oh, maybe twenty thousand feet, and open the door, and—"

"*Jonas*," Mother warned.

"I was only joking," Jonas groaned. "I don't want Pilot, anyway. If I get Pilot I'll put in an appeal."

"Come on," Mother said. She gave Lily's ribbons a final tug. "Jonas? Are you ready? Did you take your pill? I want to get a good seat in the Auditorium." She prodded Lily to the front door and Jonas followed.

It was a short ride to the Auditorium, Lily waving to her friends from her seat on the back of Mother's bicycle. Jonas stowed his bicycle beside Mother's and made his way through the throng to find his group.

The entire community attended the Ceremony each year. For the parents, it meant two days holiday from work; they sat together in the huge hall. Children sat with their groups until they went, one by one, to the stage.

Father, though, would not join Mother in the audience right away. For the earliest ceremony, the Naming, the Nurturers brought the newchildren to the stage. Jonas, from his place in the balcony with the Elevens, searched the Auditorium for a glimpse of Father. It wasn't at all hard to spot the Nurturers' section at the front; coming from it were the wails and howls of the newchildren who sat squirming on the Nurturers' laps. At every other public ceremony, the audience was silent and attentive. But once a year, they all smiled indulgently at the commotion from the little ones waiting to receive their names and families.

Jonas finally caught his father's eye and waved. Father grinned and waved back, then held up the hand of the newchild on his lap, making it wave, too.

It wasn't Gabriel. Gabe was back at the Nurturing Center today, being cared for by the night crew. He had been given an unusual and special reprieve from the committee, and granted an additional year of nurturing before his Naming and Placement. Father had gone before the committee with a plea on behalf of Gabriel, who had not yet gained the weight appropriate to his days of life nor begun to sleep soundly enough at night to be placed with his family unit. Normally such a newchild would be labeled Inadequate and released from the community.

Instead, as a result of Father's plea, Gabriel had been labeled Uncertain and given the additional year. He would continue to be nurtured at the Center and would spend his nights with Jonas's family unit. Each family member, including Lily, had been required to sign a pledge that they would not become attached to this little temporary guest, and that they would relinquish him without protest or appeal when he was assigned to his own family unit at next year's Ceremony.

At least, Jonas thought, after Gabriel was placed next year, they would still see him often because he would be part of the community. If he were released, they would not see him again. Ever. Those who were released—even as newchildren—were sent Elsewhere and never returned to the community.

Father had not had to release a single newchild this year, so Gabriel would have represented a real failure and sadness. Even Jonas, though he didn't hover over the little one the way Lily and his father did, was glad that Gabe had not been released.

The first Ceremony began right on time, and Jonas

watched as one after another each newchild was given a name and handed by the Nurturers to its new family unit. For some, it was a first child. But many came to the stage accompanied by another child beaming with pride to receive a little brother or sister, the way Jonas had when he was about to be a Five.

Asher poked Jonas's arm. "Remember when we got Phillipa?" he asked in a loud whisper. Jonas nodded. It had only been last year. Asher's parents had waited quite a long time before applying for a second child. Maybe, Jonas suspected, they had been so exhausted by Asher's lively foolishness that they had needed a little time.

Two of their group, Fiona and another female named Thea, were missing temporarily, waiting with their parents to receive newchildren. But it was rare that there was such an age gap between children in a family unit.

When her family's ceremony was completed, Fiona took the seat that had been saved for her in the row ahead of Asher and Jonas. She turned and whispered to them, "He's cute. But I don't like his name very much." She made a face and giggled. Fiona's new brother had been named Bruno. It wasn't a *great* name, Jonas thought, like—well, like Gabriel, for example. But it was okay.

The audience applause, which was enthusiastic at each Naming, rose in an exuberant swell when one parental pair, glowing with pride, took a male newchild and heard him named Caleb.

This new Caleb was a replacement child. The couple had lost their first Caleb, a cheerful little Four. Loss of a child was very, very rare. The community was extraordinarily safe, each citizen watchful and protective of all children. But somehow the first little Caleb had wandered away unnoticed, and had fallen into the river. The entire community had performed the Ceremony of Loss together, murmuring the name Caleb throughout an entire day, less and less frequently, softer in volume, as the long and somber day went on, so that the little Four seemed to fade away gradually from everyone's consciousness.

Now, at this special Naming, the community performed the brief Murmur-of-Replacement Ceremony, repeating the name for the first time since the loss: softly and slowly at first, then faster and with greater volume, as the couple stood on the stage with the newchild sleeping in the mother's arms. It was as if the first Caleb were returning.

Another newchild was given the name Roberto, and Jonas remembered that Roberto the Old had been released only last week. But there was no Murmur-of-Replacement Ceremony for the new little Roberto. Release was not the same as loss.

He sat politely through the ceremonies of Two and Three and Four, increasingly bored as he was each year. Then a break for midday meal—served outdoors—and back again to the seats, for the Fives, Sixes, Sevens, and finally, last of the first day's ceremonies, the Eights.

Jonas watched and cheered as Lily marched proudly to the stage, became an Eight and received the identifying jacket that she would wear this year, this one with smaller buttons and, for the first time, pockets, indicating that she was mature enough now to keep track of her own small belongings. She stood solemnly listening to the speech of firm instructions on the responsibilities of Eight and doing volunteer hours for the first time. But Jonas could see that Lily, though she seemed attentive, was looking longingly at the row of gleaming bicycles, which would be presented tomorrow morning to the Nines.

Next year, Lily-billy, Jonas thought.

It was an exhausting day, and even Gabriel, retrieved in his basket from the Nurturing Center, slept soundly that night.

Finally it was the morning of the Ceremony of Twelve.

Now Father sat beside Mother in the audience. Jonas could see them applauding dutifully as the Nines, one by one, wheeled their new bicycles, each with its gleaming nametag attached to the back, from the stage. He knew that his parents cringed a little, as he did, when Fritz, who lived in the dwelling next door to theirs, received his bike and almost immediately bumped into the podium with it. Fritz was a very awkward child who had been summoned for chastisement again and again. His transgressions were small ones, always: shoes on the wrong feet, schoolwork misplaced, failure to study adequately for a quiz. But each such error reflected negatively on his parents' guidance and infringed on the community's sense of order and success. Jonas and his family had not been looking forward to Fritz's bicycle, which they realized would probably too often be dropped on the front walk instead of wheeled neatly into its port.

Finally the Nines were all resettled in their seats, each having wheeled a bicycle outside where it would be waiting for its owner at the end of the day. Everyone always chuckled and made small jokes when the Nines rode home for the first time. "Want me to show you how to ride?" older friends would call. "I know you've never been on a bike before!" But invariably the grinning Nines, who in technical violation of the rule had been practicing secretly for weeks, would mount and ride off in perfect balance, training wheels never touching the ground.

Then the Tens. Jonas never found the Ceremony of Ten particularly interesting—only time-consuming, as each child's hair was snipped neatly into its distinguishing cut: females lost their braids at Ten, and males, too, relinquished their long childish hair and took on the more manly short style which exposed their ears.

Laborers moved quickly to the stage with brooms and swept away the mounds of discarded hair. Jonas could see the parents of the new Tens stir and murmur, and he knew that this evening, in many dwellings, they would be snipping and straightening the hastily done haircuts, trimming them into a neater line.

Elevens. It seemed a short time ago that Jonas had undergone the Ceremony of Eleven, but he remembered that it was not one of the more interesting ones. By Eleven, one was only waiting to be Twelve. It was simply a marking of time with no meaningful changes. There was new clothing: different undergarments for the females, whose bodies were beginning to change; and longer trousers for the males, with a specially shaped pocket for the small calculator that they would use this year in school; but those were simply presented in wrapped packages without an accompanying speech.

Break for midday meal. Jonas realized he was hungry. He and his groupmates congregated by the tables in front of the Auditorium and took their packaged food. Yesterday there had been merriment at lunch, a lot of teasing, and energy. But today the group stood anxiously separate from the other children. Jonas watched the new Nines gravitate toward their waiting bicycles, each one admiring his or her nametag. He saw the Tens stroking their new shortened hair, the females shaking their heads to feel the unaccustomed lightness without the heavy braids they had worn so long.

"I heard about a guy who was absolutely certain he was going to be assigned Engineer," Asher muttered as they ate, "and instead they gave him Sanitation Laborer. He went out the next day, jumped into the river, swam across, and joined the next community he came to. Nobody ever saw him again."

Jonas laughed. "Somebody made that story up, Ash," he said. "My father said he heard that story when *he* was a Twelve."

But Asher wasn't reassured. He was eyeing the river where it was visible behind the Auditorium. "I can't even swim very well," he said. "My swimming instructor said that I don't have the right boyishness or something."

"Buoyancy," Jonas corrected him.

"Whatever. I don't have it. I sink."

"Anyway," Jonas pointed out, "have you ever once known of anyone—I mean really known for sure, Asher, not just heard a story about it—who joined another community?"

"No," Asher admitted reluctantly. "But you can. It says so in the rules. If you don't fit in, you can apply for Elsewhere and be released. My mother says that once, about ten years ago, someone applied and was gone the next day." Then he chuckled. "She told me that because I was driving her crazy. She threatened to apply for Elsewhere."

"She was joking."

"I know. But it was true, what she said, that someone did that once. She said that it was really true. Here today and gone tomorrow. Never seen again. Not even a Ceremony of Release."

Jonas shrugged. It didn't worry him. How could someone not fit in? The community was so meticulously ordered, the choices so carefully made.

Even the Matching of Spouses was given such weighty consideration that sometimes an adult who applied to receive a spouse waited months or even *years* before a Match was approved and announced. All of the factors—disposition, energy level, intelligence, and interests—had to correspond and to interact perfectly. Jonas's mother, for example, had a higher intelligence than his father, but his father had a calmer disposition. They balanced each other. Their match, which like all Matches had been monitored by the Committee of Elders for three years before they could apply for children, had always been a successful one.

Like the Matching of Spouses and the Naming and Placement of newchildren, the Assignments were scrupulously thought through by the Committee of Elders.

He was certain that his Assignment, whatever it was to be, and Asher's too, would be the right one for them. He only wished that the midday break would conclude, that the audience would reenter the Auditorium, and the suspense would end.

As if in answer to his unspoken wish, the signal came and the crowd began to move toward the doors.

Chapter 7

Now Jonas's group had taken a new place in the Auditorium, trading with the new Elevens, so that they sat in the very front, immediately before the stage.

They were arranged by their original numbers, the numbers they had been given at birth. The numbers were rarely used after the Naming. But each child knew his number, of course. Sometimes parents used them in irritation at a child's misbehavior, indicating that mischief made one unworthy of a name. Jonas always chuckled when he heard a parent, exasperated, call sharply to a whining toddler, "That's *enough*, Twenty-three!"

Jonas was Nineteen. He had been the nineteenth newchild born his year. It had meant that at his Naming, he had been already standing and bright-eyed, soon to walk and talk. It had given him a slight advantage the first year or two, a little more maturity than many of his groupmates who had been born in the later months of that year. But it evened out, as it always did, by Three.

After Three, the children progressed at much the same level, though by their first number one could always tell who was a few months older than others in his group. Technically, Jonas's full number was Eleven-nineteen, since there were other Nineteens, of course, in each age group. And today, now that the new Elevens had been advanced this morning, there were *two* Eleven-nineteens. At the midday break he had exchanged smiles with the new one, a shy female named Harriet.

But the duplication was only for these few hours. Very soon he would not be an Eleven but a Twelve, and age would no longer matter. He would be an adult, like his parents, though a new one and untrained still.

Asher was Four, and sat now in the row ahead of Jonas. He would receive his Assignment fourth.

Fiona, Eighteen, was on his left; on his other side sat Twenty, a male named Pierre whom Jonas didn't like much. Pierre was very serious, not much fun, and a worrier and tattletale, too. "Have you checked the rules, Jonas?" Pierre was always whispering solemnly. "I'm not sure that's within the rules." Usually it was some foolish thing that no one cared about—opening his tunic if it was a day with a breeze; taking a brief try on a friend's bicycle, just to experience the different feel of it.

The initial speech at the Ceremony of Twelve was made by the Chief Elder, the leader of the community who was elected every ten years. The speech was much the same each year: recollection of the time of childhood and the period of preparation, the coming responsibilities of adult life, the profound importance of Assignment, the seriousness of training to come.

Then the Chief Elder moved ahead in her speech.

"This is the time," she began, looking directly at them, "when we acknowledge differences. You Elevens have spent all your years till now learning to fit in, to standardize your behavior, to curb any impulse that might set you apart from the group.

"But today we honor your differences. They have determined your futures."

She began to describe this year's group and its variety of personalities, though she singled no one out by name. She mentioned that there was one who had singular skills at caretaking, another who loved newchildren, one with unusual scientific aptitude, and a fourth for whom physical labor was an obvious pleasure. Jonas shifted in his seat, trying to recognize each reference as one of his groupmates. The caretaking skills were no doubt those of Fiona, on his left; he remembered noticing the tenderness with which she had bathed the Old. Probably the one with scientific aptitude was Benjamin, the male who had devised new, important equipment for the Rehabilitation Center.

He heard nothing that he recognized as himself, Jonas.

Finally the Chief Elder paid tribute to the hard work of her committee, which had performed the observations so meticulously all year. The Committee of Elders stood and was acknowledged by applause. Jonas noticed Asher yawn slightly, covering his mouth politely with his hand.

Then, at last, the Chief Elder called number One to the stage, and the Assignments began.

Each announcement was lengthy, accompanied by a speech directed at the new Twelve. Jonas tried to pay attention as One, smiling happily, received her Assignment as Fish Hatchery Attendant along with words of praise for her childhood spent doing many volunteer hours there, and her obvious interest in the important process of providing nourishment for the community.

Number One—her name was Madeline—returned, finally, amidst applause to her seat, wearing the new badge that designated her Fish Hatchery Attendant. Jonas was certainly glad that *that* Assignment was taken; he wouldn't have wanted it. But he gave Madeline a smile of congratulation.

When Two, a female named Inger, received her

Assignment as Birthmother, Jonas remembered that his mother had called it a job without honor. But he thought that the committee had chosen well. Inger was a nice girl though somewhat lazy, and her body was strong. She would enjoy the three years of being pampered that would follow her brief training; she would give birth easily and well; and the task of Laborer that would follow would use her strength, keep her healthy, and impose self-discipline. Inger was smiling when she resumed her seat. Birthmother was an important job, if lacking in prestige.

Jonas noticed that Asher looked nervous. He kept turning his head and glancing back at Jonas until the group leader had to give him a silent chastisement, a motion to sit still and face forward.

Three, Isaac, was given an Assignment as Instructor of Sixes, which obviously pleased him and was well deserved. Now there were three Assignments gone, none of them ones that Jonas would have liked—not that he could have been a Birthmother, anyway, he realized with amusement. He tried to sort through the list in his mind, the possible Assignments that remained. But there were so many he gave it up; and anyway, now it was Asher's turn. He paid strict attention as his friend went to the stage and stood self-consciously beside the Chief Elder.

"All of us in the community know and enjoy Asher," the Chief Elder began. Asher grinned and scratched one leg with the other foot. The audience chuckled softly.

"When the committee began to consider Asher's Assignment," she went on, "there were some possibilities that were immediately discarded. Some that would clearly not have been right for Asher.

"For example," she said, smiling, "we did not

consider for an instant designating Asher an Instructor of Threes."

The audience howled with laughter. Asher laughed, too, looking sheepish but pleased at the special attention. The Instructors of Threes were in charge of the acquisition of correct language.

"In fact," the Chief Elder continued, chuckling a little to herself, "we even gave a little thought to some retroactive chastisement for the one who had been *Asher's* Instructor of Threes so long ago. At the meeting where Asher was discussed, we retold many of the stories that we all remembered from his days of language acquisition.

"Especially," she said, chuckling, "the difference between snack and smack. Remember, Asher?"

Asher nodded ruefully, and the audience laughed aloud. Jonas did, too. He remembered, though he had been only a Three at the time himself.

The punishment used for small children was a regulated system of smacks with the discipline wand: a thin, flexible weapon that stung painfully when it was wielded. The Childcare specialists were trained very carefully in the discipline methods: a quick smack across the hands for a bit of minor misbehavior, three sharper smacks on the bare legs for a second offense.

Poor Asher, who always talked too fast and mixed up words, even as a toddler. As a Three, eager for his juice and crackers at snacktime, he one day said "smack" instead of "snack" as he stood waiting in line for the morning treat.

Jonas remembered it clearly. He could still see little Asher, wiggling with impatience in the line. He remembered the cheerful voice call out, "I want my smack!"

The other Threes, including Jonas, had laughed

nervously. "Snack!" they corrected. "You meant snack, Asher!" But the mistake had been made. And precision of language was one of the most important tasks of small children. Asher had asked for a smack.

The discipline wand, in the hand of the Childcare worker, whistled as it came down across Asher's hands. Asher whimpered, cringed, and corrected himself instantly. "Snack," he whispered.

But the next morning he had done it again. And again the following week. He couldn't seem to stop, though for each lapse the discipline wand came again, escalating to a series of painful lashes that left marks on Asher's legs. Eventually, for a period of time, Asher stopped talking altogether, when he was a Three.

"For a while," the Chief Elder said, relating the story, "we had a silent Asher! But he learned."

She turned to him with a smile. "When he began to talk again, it was with greater precision. And now his lapses are very few. His corrections and apologies are very prompt. And his good humor is unfailing." The audience murmured in agreement. Asher's cheerful disposition was well-known throughout the community.

"Asher." She lifted her voice to make the official announcement. "We have given you the Assignment of Assistant Director of Recreation."

She clipped on his new badge as he stood beside her, beaming. Then he turned and left the stage as the audience cheered. When he had taken his seat again, the Chief Elder looked down at him and said the words that she had said now four times, and would say to each new Twelve. Somehow she gave it special meaning for each of them.

"Asher," she said, "thank you for your childhood."

The Assignments continued, and Jonas watched and listened, relieved now by the wonderful Assignment his best friend had been given. But he was more and more apprehensive as his own approached. Now the new Twelves in the row ahead had all received their badges. They were fingering them as they sat, and Jonas knew that each one was thinking about the training that lay ahead. For some—one studious male had been selected as Doctor, a female as Engineer, and another for Law and Justice—it would be years of hard work and study. Others, like Laborers and Birthmothers, would have a much shorter training period.

Eighteen, Fiona, on his left, was called. Jonas knew she must be nervous, but Fiona was a calm female. She had been sitting quietly, serenely, throughout the Ceremony.

Even the applause, though enthusiastic, seemed serene when Fiona was given the important Assignment of Caretaker of the Old. It was perfect for such a sensitive, gentle girl, and her smile was satisfied and pleased when she took her seat beside him again.

Jonas prepared himself to walk to the stage when the applause ended and the Chief Elder picked up the next folder and looked down to the group to call forward the next new Twelve. He was calm now that his turn had come. He took a deep breath and smoothed his hair with his hand.

"Twenty," he heard her voice say clearly. "Pierre."

She *skipped* me, Jonas thought, stunned. Had he heard wrong? No. There was a sudden hush in the crowd, and he knew that the entire community realized that the Chief Elder had moved from Eighteen to Twenty, leaving a gap. On his right, Pierre, with a startled look, rose from his seat and moved to the stage.

A mistake. She made a mistake. But Jonas knew, even as he had the thought, that she hadn't. The Chief Elder made no mistakes. Not at the Ceremony of Twelve.

He felt dizzy, and couldn't focus his attention. He didn't hear what Assignment Pierre received, and was only dimly aware of the applause as the boy returned, wearing his new badge. Then: Twenty-one. Twenty-two.

The numbers continued in order. Jonas sat, dazed, as they moved into the Thirties and then the Forties, nearing the end. Each time, at each announcement, his heart jumped for a moment, and he thought wild thoughts. Perhaps now she would call his name. Could he have forgotten his own number? No. He had always been Nineteen. He was sitting in the seat marked Nineteen.

But she had *skipped* him. He saw the others in his group glance at him, embarrassed, and then avert their eyes quickly. He saw a worried look on the face of his group leader.

He hunched his shoulders and tried to make himself smaller in the seat. He wanted to disappear, to fade away, not to exist. He didn't dare to turn and find his parents in the crowd. He couldn't bear to see their faces darkened with shame.

Jonas bowed his head and searched through his mind. *What had he done wrong?*

Chapter 8

The audience was clearly ill at ease. They applauded at the final Assignment, but the applause was piecemeal, no longer a crescendo of united enthusiasm. There were murmurs of confusion.

Jonas moved his hands together, clapping, but it was an automatic, meaningless gesture that he wasn't even aware of. His mind had shut out all of the earlier emotions: the anticipation, excitement, pride, and even the happy kinship with his friends. Now he felt only humiliation and terror.

The Chief Elder waited until the uneasy applause subsided. Then she spoke again.

"I know," she said in her vibrant, gracious voice, "that you are all concerned. That you feel I have made a mistake."

She smiled. The community, relieved from its discomfort very slightly by her benign statement, seemed to breathe more easily. It was very silent.

Jonas looked up.

"I have caused you anxiety," she said. "I apologize to my community." Her voice flowed over the assembled crowd.

"We accept your apology," they all uttered together.

"Jonas," she said, looking down at him, "I apologize to you in particular. I caused you anguish."

"I accept your apology," Jonas replied shakily.

"Please come to the stage now."

Earlier that day, dressing in his own dwelling, he had practiced the kind of jaunty, self-assured walk that he hoped he could make to the stage when his turn came. All of that was forgotten now. He simply willed himself to stand, to move his feet that felt weighted and clumsy, to go forward, up the steps and across the platform until he stood at her side.

Reassuringly she placed her arm across his tense shoulders.

"Jonas has not been assigned," she informed the crowd, and his heart sank.

Then she went on. "Jonas has been *selected.*"

He blinked. What did that mean? He felt a collective, questioning stir from the audience. They, too, were puzzled.

In a firm, commanding voice she announced, "Jonas has been selected to be our next Receiver of Memory."

Then he heard the gasp—the sudden intake of breath, drawn sharply in astonishment, by each of the seated Citizens. He saw their faces; the eyes widened in awe.

And still he did not understand.

"Such a selection is very, very rare," the Chief Elder told the audience. "Our community has only one Receiver. It is he who trains his successor.

"We have had our current Receiver for a very long time," she went on. Jonas followed her eyes and saw that she was looking at one of the Elders. The Committee of Elders was sitting together in a group; and the Chief Elder's eyes were now on one who sat in the midst but seemed oddly separate from them. It was a man Jonas had never noticed before, a bearded man with pale eyes. He was watching Jonas intently.

"We failed in our last selection," the Chief Elder said solemnly. "It was ten years ago, when Jonas was just a toddler. I will not dwell on the experience because it causes us all terrible discomfort."

Jonas didn't know what she was referring to, but

he could sense the discomfort of the audience. they shifted uneasily in their seats.

"We have not been hasty this time," she continued. "We could not afford another failure."

"Sometimes," she went on, speaking now in a lighter tone, relaxing the tension in the Auditorium, "we are not entirely certain about the Assignments, even after the most painstaking observations. Sometimes we worry that the one assigned might not develop, through training, every attribute necessary. Elevens are still children, after all. What we observe as playfulness and patience—the requirements to become Nurturer—could, with maturity, be revealed as simply foolishness and indolence. So we continue to observe during training, and to modify behavior when necessary.

"But the Receiver-in-training cannot be observed, cannot be modified. That is stated quite clearly in the rules. He is to be alone, apart, while he is prepared by the current Receiver for the job which is the most honored in our community."

Alone? Apart? Jonas listened with increasing unease.

"Therefore the selection must be sound. It must be a unanimous choice of the Committee. They can have no doubts, however fleeting. If, during the process, an Elder reports a dream of uncertainty, that dream has the power to set a candidate aside instantly.

"Jonas was identified as a possible Receiver many years ago. We have observed him meticulously. There were no dreams of uncertainty.

"He has shown all of the qualities that a Receiver must have."

With her hand still firmly on his shoulder, the Chief Elder listed the qualities.

"*Intelligence,*" she said. " We are all aware that Jonas has been a top student throughout his school days.

"*Integrity,*" she said next. "Jonas has, like all of us, committed minor transgressions." She smiled at him. "We expect that. We hoped, also, that he would present himself promptly for chastisement, and he has always done so.

"*Courage,*" she went on. "Only one of us here today has ever undergone the rigorous training required of a Receiver. He, of course, is the most important member of the committee: the current Receiver. It was he who reminded us, again and again, of the courage required.

"Jonas," she said, turning to him, but speaking in a voice that the entire community could hear, "the training required of you involves pain. Physical pain."

He felt his heart flutter within him.

"You have never experienced that. Yes, you have scraped your knees in falls from your bicycle. Yes, you crushed your finger in a door last year."

Jonas nodded, agreeing, as he recalled the incident, and its accompanying misery.

"But you will be faced, now," she explained gently, "with pain of a magnitude that none of us here can comprehend because it is beyond our experience. The Receiver himself was not able to describe it, only to remind us that you would be faced with it, that you would need immense courage. We cannot prepare you for that.

"But we feel certain that you are brave," she said to him.

He did not feel brave at all. Not now.

"The fourth essential attribute," the Chief Elder said, "is *wisdom*. Jonas has not yet acquired that.

The acquisition of wisdom will come through his training.

"We are convinced that Jonas has the ability to acquire wisdom. That is what we looked for.

"Finally, The Receiver must have one more quality, and it is one which I can only name, but not describe. I do not understand it. You members of the community will not understand it, either. Perhaps Jonas will, because the current Receiver has told us that Jonas already has this quality. He calls it the Capacity to See Beyond."

The Chief Elder looked at Jonas with a question in her eyes. The audience watched him, too. They were silent.

For a moment he froze, consumed with despair. He *didn't* have it, the whatever-she-had-said. He didn't know what it was. Now was the moment when he would have to confess, to say, "No, I don't. I *can't*," and throw himself on their mercy, ask their forgiveness, to explain that he had been wrongly chosen, that he was not the right one at all.

But when he looked out across the crowd, the sea of faces, the thing happened again. The thing that had happened with the apple.

They *changed*.

He blinked, and it was gone. His shoulders straightened slightly. Briefly he felt a tiny sliver of sureness for the first time.

She was still watching him. They all were.

"I think it's true," he told the Chief Elder and the community. "I don't understand it yet. I don't know what it is. But sometimes I see something. And maybe it's beyond."

She took her arm from his shoulders.

"Jonas," she said, speaking not to him alone but to the entire community of which he was a part, "you will be trained to be our next Receiver of Memory. We thank you for your childhood."

Then she turned and left the stage, left him there alone, standing and facing the crowd, which began spontaneously the collective murmur of his name.

"Jonas." It was a whisper at first: hushed, barely audible. "Jonas. Jonas."

Then louder, faster. "**JONAS. JONAS. JONAS.**"

With the chant, Jonas knew, the community was accepting him and his new role, giving him life, the way they had given it to the newchild Caleb. His heart swelled with gratitude and pride.

But at the same time he was filled with fear. He did not know what his selection meant. He did not know what he was to become.

Or what would become of him.

Chapter 9

Now, for the first time in his twelve years of life, Jonas felt separate, different. He remembered what the Chief Elder had said: that his training would be alone and apart.

But his training had not yet begun and already, upon leaving the Auditorium, he felt the apartness. Holding the folder she had given him, he made his way through the throng, looking for his family unit and for Asher. People moved aside for him. They watched him. He thought he could hear whispers.

"Ash!" he called, spotting his friend near the rows of bicycles. "Ride back with me?"

"Sure." Asher smiled, his usual smile, friendly and familiar. But Jonas felt a moment of hesitation from his friend, an uncertainty.

"Congratulations," Asher said.

"You too," Jonas replied. "It was really funny, when she told about the smacks. You got more applause than almost anybody else."

The other new Twelves clustered nearby, placing their folders carefully into the carrying containers on the backs of the bikes. In each dwelling tonight they would be studying the instructions for the beginning of their training. Each night for years the children had memorized the required lessons for school, often yawning with boredom. Tonight they would all begin eagerly to memorize the rules for their adult Assignments.

"Congratulations, Asher!" someone called. Then that hesitation again. "You too, Jonas!"

Asher and Jonas responded with congratulations

to their groupmates. Jonas saw his parents watching him from the place where their own bicycles were waiting. Lily had already been strapped into her seat.

He waved. They waved back, smiling, but he noticed that Lily was watching him solemnly, her thumb in her mouth.

He rode directly to his dwelling, exchanging only small jokes and unimportant remarks with Asher.

"See you in the morning, Recreation Director!" he called, dismounting by his door as Asher continued on.

"Right! See you!" Asher called back. Once again, there was just a moment when things weren't quite the same, weren't quite as they had always been through the long friendship. Perhaps he had imagined it. Things couldn't change, with Asher.

The evening meal was quieter than usual. Lily chattered about her plans for volunteer work; she would begin, she said, at the Nurturing Center, since she was already an expert at feeding Gabriel.

"I know," she added quickly, when her father gave her a warning glance, "I won't mention his name. I know I'm not supposed to know his name.

"I can't wait for tomorrow to come," she said happily.

Jonas sighed uneasily. "I can," he muttered.

"You've been greatly honored," his mother said. "Your father and I are very proud."

"It's the most important job in the community," Father said.

"But just the other night, you said that the job of making Assignments was the most important!"

Mother nodded. "This is different. It's not a *job*, really. I never thought, never expected—" She paused. "There's only one Receiver."

"But the Chief Elder said that they had made a

selection before, and that it failed. What was she talking about?"

Both of his parents hesitated. Finally his father described the previous selection. "It was very much as it was today, Jonas—the same suspense, as one Eleven had been passed over when the Assignments were given. Then the announcement, when they singled out the one—"

Jonas interrupted. "What was his name?"

His mother replied, "Her, not his. It was a female. But we are never to speak the name, or to use it again for a newchild."

Jonas was shocked. A name designated Not-to-Be-Spoken indicated the highest degree of disgrace.

"What happened to her?" he asked nervously.

But his parents looked blank. "We don't know," his father said uncomfortably. "We never saw her again."

A silence fell over the room. They looked at each other. Finally his mother, rising from the table, said, "You've been greatly honored, Jonas. Greatly honored."

Alone in his sleeping room, prepared for bed, Jonas opened his folder at last. Some of the other Twelves, he had noticed, had been given folders thick with printed pages. He imagined Benjamin, the scientific male in his group, beginning to read pages of rules and instructions with relish. He pictured Fiona smiling her gentle smile as she bent over the lists of duties and methods that she would be required to learn in the days to come.

But his own folder was startlingly close to empty. Inside there was only a single printed sheet. He read it twice.

JONAS
RECEIVER OF MEMORY

1. Go immediately at the end of school hours each day to the Annex entrance behind the House of the Old and present yourself to the attendant.

2. Go immediately to your dwelling at the conclusion of Training Hours each day.

3. From this moment you are exempted from rules governing rudeness. You may ask any question of any citizen and you will receive answers.

4. Do not discuss your training with any other member of the community, including parents and Elders.

5. From this moment you are prohibited from dream-telling.

6. Except for illness or injury unrelated to your training, do not apply for any medication.

7. You are not permitted to apply for release.

8. You may lie.

Jonas was stunned. What would happen to his friendships? His mindless hours playing ball, or riding his bike along the river? Those had been happy and vital times for him. Were they to be completely taken from him, now? The simple logistic instructions—where to go, and when—were expected. Every Twelve had to be told, of course, where and how and when to report for training. But he was a little dismayed that his schedule left no time, apparently, for recreation.

The exemption from rudeness startled him. Reading it again, however, he realized that it didn't compel him to be rude; it simply allowed him the option. He was quite certain he would never take advantage of it. He was so completely, so thoroughly accustomed to courtesy within the community that the thought of asking another citizen an intimate question, of calling someone's attention to an area of awkwardness, was unnerving.

The prohibition of dream-telling, he thought, would not be a real problem. He dreamed so rarely that the dream-telling did not come easily to him anyway, and he was glad to be excused from it. He wondered briefly, though, how to deal with it at the morning meal. What if he *did* dream—should he simply tell his family unit, as he did so often, anyway, that he hadn't? That would be a lie. Still, the final rule said . . . well, he wasn't quite ready to think about the final rule on the page.

The restriction of medication unnerved him. Medication was always available to citizens, even to children, through their parents. When he had crushed his finger in the door, he had quickly, gasping into the speaker, notified his mother; she had hastily requisitioned relief-of-pain medication which had promptly been delivered to his dwelling. Almost instantly the excruciating pain in his hand had diminished to the throb which was, now, all he could recall of the experience.

Re-reading rule number 6, he realized that a crushed finger fell into the category of "unrelated to training." So if it ever happened again—and he was quite certain it wouldn't; he had been very careful near heavy doors since the accident!—he could still receive medication.

The pill he took now, each morning, was also unrelated to training. So he would continue to receive the pill.

But he remembered uneasily what the Chief Elder had said about the pain that would come with his training. She had called it indescribable.

Jonas swallowed hard, trying without success to imagine what such pain might be like, with no medication at all. But it was beyond his comprehension.

He felt no reaction to rule number 7 at all. It had never occurred to him that under any circumstances, ever, he might apply for release.

Finally he steeled himself to read the final rule again. He had been trained since earliest childhood, since his earliest learning of language, never to lie. It was an integral part of the learning of precise speech. Once, when he had been a Four, he had said, just prior to the midday meal at school, "I'm starving."

Immediately he had been taken aside for a brief private lesson in language precision. He was not starving, it was pointed out. He was *hungry*. No one in the community was starving, had ever been starving, would ever be starving. To say "starving" was to speak a lie. An unintentional lie, of course. But the reason for precision of language was to ensure that unintentional lies were never uttered. Did he understand that? they asked him. And he had.

He had never, within his memory, been tempted to lie. Asher did not lie. Lily did not lie. His parents did not lie. No one did. Unless . . .

Now Jonas had a thought that he had never had before. This new thought was frightening. What if *others*—*adults*—had, upon becoming Twelves, received in *their* instructions the same terrifying sentence?

What if they had all been instructed: *You may lie?*

His mind reeled. Now, empowered to ask questions of utmost rudeness—and promised answers—he *could,* conceivably (though it was almost unimaginable), ask someone, some adult, his father perhaps: "Do you lie?"

But he would have no way of knowing if the answer he received were true.

Chapter 10

"I go in here, Jonas," Fiona told him when they reached the front door of the House of the Old after parking their bicycles in the designated area.

"I don't know why I'm nervous," she confessed. "I've been here so often before." She turned her folder over in her hands.

"Well, everything's different now," Jonas reminded her.

"Even the nameplates on our bikes," Fiona laughed. During the night the nameplate of each new Twelve had been removed by the Maintenance Crew and replaced with the style that indicated citizen-in-training.

"I don't want to be late," she said hastily, and started up the steps. "If we finish at the same time, I'll ride home with you."

Jonas nodded, waved to her, and headed around the building toward the Annex, a small wing attached to the back. He certainly didn't want to be late for his first day of training, either.

The Annex was very ordinary, its door unremarkable. He reached for the heavy handle, then noticed a buzzer on the wall. So he buzzed instead.

"Yes?" The voice came through a small speaker above the buzzer.

"It's, uh, Jonas. I'm the new—I mean—"

"Come in." A click indicated that the door had been unlatched.

The lobby was very small and contained only a desk at which a female Attendant sat working on some papers. She looked up when he entered; then, to his surprise, she stood. It was a small thing, the standing; but no one had ever stood automatically to acknowledge Jonas's presence before.

"Welcome, Receiver of Memory," she said respectfully.

"Oh, please," he replied uncomfortably. "Call me Jonas."

She smiled, pushed a button, and he heard a click that unlocked the door to her left. "You may go right on in," she told him.

Then she seemed to notice his discomfort and to realize its origin. No doors in the community were locked, ever. None that Jonas knew of, anyway.

"The locks are simply to insure The Receiver's privacy because he needs concentration," she explained. "It would be difficult if citizens wandered in, looking for the Department of Bicycle Repair, or something."

Jonas laughed, relaxing a little. The woman seemed very friendly, and it was true—in fact it was a joke throughout the community—that the Department of Bicycle Repair, an unimportant little office, was relocated so often that no one ever knew where it was.

"There is nothing dangerous here," she told him.

"But," she added, glancing at the wall clock, "he doesn't like to be kept waiting."

Jonas hurried through the door and found himself in a comfortably furnished living area. It was not unlike his own family unit's dwelling. Furniture was standard throughout the community: practical, sturdy, the function of each piece clearly defined. A bed for sleeping. A table for eating. A desk for studying.

All of those things were in this spacious room, though each was slightly different from those in his own dwelling. The fabrics on the upholstered chairs and sofa were slightly thicker and more luxurious; the table legs were not straight like those at home, but slender and curved, with a small carved decoration at the foot. The bed, in an alcove at the far end of the room, was draped with a splendid cloth embroidered over its entire surface with intricate designs.

But the most conspicuous difference was the books. In his own dwelling, there were the necessary reference volumes that each household contained: a dictionary, and the thick community volume which contained descriptions of every office, factory, building, and committee. And the Book of Rules, of course.

The books in his own dwelling were the only books that Jonas had ever seen. He had never known that other books existed.

But this room's walls were completely covered by bookcases, filled, which reached to the ceiling. There must have been hundreds—perhaps thousands—of books, their titles embossed in shiny letters.

Jonas stared at them. He couldn't imagine what the thousands of pages contained. Could there be rules beyond the rules that governed the community? Could there be more descriptions of offices and factories and committees?

He had only a second to look around because he was aware that the man sitting in a chair beside the table was watching him. Hastily he moved forward, stood before the man, bowed slightly, and said, "I'm Jonas."

"I know. Welcome, Receiver of Memory."

Jonas recognized the man. He was the Elder who had seemed separate from the others at the Ceremony, though he was dressed in the same special clothing that only Elders wore.

Jonas looked self-consciously into the pale eyes that mirrored his own.

"Sir, I apologize for my lack of understanding. . . . "

He waited, but the man did not give the standard accepting-of-apology response.

After a moment, Jonas went on, "But I thought— I mean I *think*," he corrected, reminding himself that if precision of language were ever to be important, it was certainly important *now*, in the presence of this man, "that you are the Receiver of Memory. I'm only, well, I was only assigned, I mean selected, yesterday. I'm not anything at all. Not yet."

The man looked at him thoughtfully, silently. It was a look that combined interest, curiosity, concern, and perhaps a little sympathy as well.

Finally he spoke. "Beginning today, this moment, at least to me, you are the Receiver.

"I have been the Receiver for a long time. A very, very long time. You can see that, can't you?"

Jonas nodded. The man was wrinkled, and his eyes, though piercing in their unusual lightness, seemed tired. The flesh around them was darkened into shadowed circles.

"I can see that you are very old," Jonas responded with respect. The Old were always given the highest respect.

The man smiled. He touched the sagging flesh on his own face with amusement. "I am not, actually, as old as I look," he told Jonas. "This job has aged me. I know I look as if I should be scheduled for release very soon. But actually I have a good deal of time left.

"I was pleased, though, when you were selected. It took them a long time. The failure of the previous selection was ten years ago, and my energy is starting to diminish. I need what strength I have remaining for your training. We have hard and painful work to do, you and I.

"Please sit down," he said, and gestured toward the nearby chair. Jonas lowered himself onto the soft cushioned seat.

The man closed his eyes and continued speaking. "When I became a Twelve, I was selected, as you were. I was frightened, as I'm sure you are." He opened his eyes for a moment and peered at Jonas, who nodded.

The eyes closed again. "I came to this very room to begin my training. It was such a long time ago.

"The previous Receiver seemed just as old to me as I do to you. He was just as tired as I am today."

He sat forward suddenly, opened his eyes, and said, "You may ask questions. I have so little experience in describing this process. It is forbidden to talk of it."

"I know, sir. I have read the instructions," Jonas said.

"So I may neglect to make things as clear as I should."

The man chuckled. "My job is important and has enormous honor. But that does not mean I am perfect, and when I tried before to train a successor, I failed. Please ask any questions that will help you."

In his mind, Jonas had questions. A thousand. A *million* questions. As many questions as there were books lining the walls. But he did not ask one, not yet.

The man sighed, seeming to put his thoughts in order. Then he spoke again. "Simply stated," he said, "although it's not really simple at all, my job is to transmit to you all the memories I have within me. Memories of the past."

"Sir," Jonas said tentatively, "I would be very

interested to hear the story of your life, and to listen to your memories.

"I apologize for interrupting," he added quickly.

The man waved his hand impatiently. "No apologies in this room. We haven't time."

"Well," Jonas went on, uncomfortably aware that he might be interrupting again, "I am really interested, I don't mean that I'm not. But I don't exactly understand why it's so important. I could do some adult job in the community, and in my recreation time I could come and listen to the stories from your childhood. I'd like that. Actually," he added, "I've done that already, in the House of the Old. The Old like to tell about their childhoods, and it's always fun to listen."

The man shook his head. "No, no," he said. "I'm not being clear. It's not my past, not my childhood that I must transmit to you."

He leaned back, resting his head against the back of the upholstered chair. "It's the memories of the whole world," he said with a sigh. "Before you, before me, before the previous Receiver, and generations before him."

Jonas frowned. "The whole world?" he asked. "I don't understand. Do you mean not just us? Not just the community? Do you mean Elsewhere, too?" He tried, in his mind, to grasp the concept. "I'm sorry, sir. I don't understand exactly. Maybe I'm not smart enough. I don't know what you mean when you say 'the whole world' or 'generations before him.' I thought there was only us. I thought there was only now."

"There's much more. There's all that goes beyond—all that is Elsewhere—and all that goes back, and back, and back. I received all of those, when I was selected. And here in this room, all alone,

I re-experience them again and again. It is how wisdom comes. And how we shape our future."

He rested for a moment, breathing deeply. "I am so *weighted* with them," he said.

Jonas felt a terrible concern for the man, suddenly.

"It's as if . . ." The man paused, seeming to search his mind for the right words of description. "It's like going downhill through deep snow on a sled," he said, finally. "At first it's exhilarating: the speed, the sharp, clear air, but then the snow accumulates, builds up on the runners, and you slow, you have to push hard to keep going, and—"

He shook his head suddenly, and peered at Jonas. "That meant nothing to you, did it?" he asked.

Jonas was confused. "I didn't understand it, sir."

"Of course you didn't. You don't know what snow is, do you?"

Jonas shook his head.

"Or a sled? Runners?"

"No, sir," Jonas said.

"Downhill? The term means nothing to you?"

"Nothing, sir."

"Well, it's a place to start. I'd been wondering how to begin. Move to the bed, and lie face down. Remove your tunic first."

Jonas did so, a little apprehensively. Beneath his bare chest, he felt the soft folds of the magnificent cloth that covered the bed. He watched as the man rose and moved first to the wall where the speaker was. It was the same sort of speaker that occupied a place in every dwelling, but one thing about it was different. This one had a switch, which the man deftly snapped to the end that said OFF.

Jonas almost gasped aloud. To have the power to turn the speaker *off!* It was an astonishing thing.

Then the man moved with surprising quickness to

the corner where the bed was. He sat on a chair beside Jonas, who was motionless, waiting for what would happen next.

"Close your eyes. Relax. This will not be painful."

Jonas remembered that he was allowed, that he had even been encouraged, to ask questions. "What are you going to do, sir?" he asked, hoping that his voice didn't betray his nervousness.

"I am going to transmit the memory of snow," the old man said, and placed his hands on Jonas's bare back.

Chapter 11

Jonas felt nothing unusual at first. He felt only the light touch of the old man's hands on his back.

He tried to relax, to breathe evenly. The room was absolutely silent, and for a moment Jonas feared that he might disgrace himself now, on the first day of his training, by falling asleep.

Then he shivered. He realized that the touch of the hands felt, suddenly, cold. At the same instant, breathing in, he felt the air change, and his very breath was cold. He licked his lips, and in doing so, his tongue touched the suddenly chilled air.

It was very startling; but he was not at all frightened, now. He was filled with energy, and he breathed again, feeling the sharp intake of frigid air. Now, too, he could feel cold air swirling around his entire body. He felt it blow against his hands where they lay at his sides, and over his back.

The touch of the man's hands seemed to have disappeared.

Now he became aware of an entirely new sensation: pinpricks? No, because they were soft and without pain. Tiny, cold, featherlike feelings peppered his body and face. He put out his tongue again, and caught one of the dots of cold upon it. It disappeared from his awareness instantly, but he caught another, and another. The sensation made him smile.

One part of his consciousness knew that he was still lying there, on the bed, in the Annex room. Yet another, separate part of his being was upright now, in a sitting position, and beneath him he could feel that he was not on the soft decorated bedcovering at all, but rather seated on a flat, hard surface. His hands now held (though at the same time they were still motionless at his sides) a rough, damp rope.

And he could *see,* though his eyes were closed. He could see a bright, whirling torrent of crystals in the air around him, and he could see them gather on the backs of his hands, like cold fur.

His breath was visible.

Beyond, through the swirl of what he now, somehow, perceived was the thing the old man had spoken of—*snow*—he could look out and down a great distance. He was up high someplace. The ground was thick with the furry snow, but he sat slightly above it on a hard, flat object.

Sled, he knew abruptly. He was sitting on a thing called sled. And the sled itself seemed to be poised at the top of a long, extended mound that rose from the very land where he was. Even as he thought the word "mound" his new consciousness told him *hill.*

Then the sled, with Jonas himself upon it, began to move through the snowfall, and he understood instantly that now he was going downhill. No voice made an explanation. The experience explained itself to him.

His face cut through the frigid air as he began the descent, moving through the substance called snow on the vehicle called sled, which propelled itself on what he now knew without doubt to be *runners.*

Comprehending all of those things as he sped downward, he was free to enjoy the breathless glee that overwhelmed him: the speed, the clear cold air, the total silence, the feeling of balance and excitement and peace.

Then, as the angle of incline lessened, as the mound—the *hill*—flattened, nearing the bottom, the sled's forward motion slowed. The snow was piled now around it, and he pushed with his body, moving it forward, not wanting the exhilarating ride to end.

Finally the obstruction of the piled snow was too much for the thin runners of the sled, and he came to a stop. He sat there for a moment, panting, holding the rope in his cold hands. Tentatively he opened his eyes—not his snow-hill-sled eyes, for they had been open throughout the strange ride. He opened his ordinary eyes, and saw that he was still on the bed, that he had not moved at all.

The old man, still beside the bed, was watching him. "How do you feel?" he asked.

Jonas sat up and tried to answer honestly. "Surprised," he said, after a moment.

The old man wiped his forehead with his sleeve. "Whew," he said. "It was exhausting. But you know, even transmitting that tiny memory to you—I think it lightened me just a little."

"Do you mean—you did say I could ask questions?"

The man nodded, encouraging his question.

"Do you mean that now you don't have the memory of it—of that ride on the sled—anymore?"

"That's right. A little weight off this old body."

"But it was such fun! And now you don't have it anymore! I *took* it from you!"

But the old man laughed. "All I gave you was one ride, on one sled, in one snow, on one hill. I have a whole world of them in my memory. I could give them to you one by one, a thousand times, and there would still be more."

"Are you saying that I—I mean we—could do it again?" Jonas asked. "I'd really like to. I think I could steer, by pulling the rope. I didn't try this time, because it was so new."

The old man, laughing, shook his head. "Maybe another day, for a treat. But there's no time, really, just to play. I only wanted to begin by showing you how it works.

"Now," he said, turning businesslike, "lie back down. I want to—"

Jonas did. He was eager for whatever experience would come next. But he had, suddenly, so many questions.

"Why don't we have snow, and sleds, and hills?" he asked. "And when did we, in the past? Did my parents have sleds when they were young? Did you?"

The old man shrugged and gave a short laugh. "No," he told Jonas. "It's a very distant memory. That's why it was so exhausting—I had to tug it forward from many generations back. It was given to me when I was a new Receiver, and the previous Receiver had to pull it through a long time period, too."

"But what happened to those things? Snow, and the rest of it?"

"Climate Control. Snow made growing food difficult, limited the agricultural periods. And unpredictable weather made transportation almost impossible at times. It wasn't a practical thing, so it became obsolete when we went to Sameness.

"And hills, too," he added. "They made conveyance of goods unwieldy. Trucks; buses. Slowed them down. So—" He waved his hand, as if a gesture had caused hills to disappear. "Sameness," he concluded.

Jonas frowned. "I wish we had those things, still. Just now and then."

The old man smiled. "So do I," he said. "But that choice is not ours."

"But sir," Jonas suggested, "since you have so much power—"

The man corrected him. "Honor," he said firmly. "I have great honor. So will you. But you will find that that is not the same as power.

"Lie quietly now. Since we've entered into the topic of climate, let me give you something else. And this time I'm not going to tell you the name of it, because I want to test the receiving. You should be able to perceive the name without being told. I gave away snow and sled and downhill and runners by telling them to you in advance."

Without being instructed, Jonas closed his eyes again. He felt the hands on his back again. He waited.

Now it came more quickly, the feelings. This time the hands didn't become cold, but instead began to feel warm on his body. They moistened a little. The warmth spread, extending across his shoulders, up his neck, onto the side of his face. He could feel it through his clothed parts, too: a pleasant, all-over sensation; and when he licked his lips this time, the air was hot and heavy.

He didn't move. There was no sled. His posture didn't change. He was simply alone someplace, out of doors, lying down, and the warmth came from far above. It was not as exciting as the ride through the snowy air; but it was pleasurable and comforting.

Suddenly he perceived the word for it: *sunshine*. He perceived that it came from the sky.

Then it ended.

"Sunshine," he said aloud, opening his eyes.

"Good. You did get the word. That makes my job easier. Not so much explaining."

"And it came from the sky."

"That's right," the old man said. "Just the way it used to."

"Before Sameness. Before Climate Control," Jonas added.

The man laughed. "You receive well, and learn quickly. I'm very pleased with you. That's enough for today, I think. We're off to a good start."

There was a question bothering Jonas. "Sir," he said, "the Chief Elder told me—she told everyone—and you told me, too, that it would be painful. So I was a little scared. But it didn't hurt at all. I really enjoyed it." He looked quizzically at the old man.

The man sighed. "I started you with memories of pleasure. My previous failure gave me the wisdom to do that." He took a few deep breaths. "Jonas," he said, "it will be painful. But it need not be painful yet."

"I'm brave. I really am." Jonas sat up a little straighter.

The old man looked at him for a moment. He smiled. "I can see that," he said. "Well, since you asked the question—I think I have enough energy for one more transmission."

"Lie down once more. This will be the last today."

Jonas obeyed cheerfully. He closed his eyes, waiting, and felt the hands again; then he felt the warmth again, the sunshine again, coming from the sky of this other consciousness that was so new to him. This time, as he lay basking in the wonderful warmth, he felt the passage of time. His real self was aware that it was only a minute or two; but his other, memory-receiving self felt hours pass in the sun. His skin began to sting. Restlessly he moved one arm, bending it, and felt a sharp pain in the crease of his inner arm at the elbow.

"Ouch," he said loudly, and shifted on the bed. "Owwww," he said, wincing at the shift, and even moving his mouth to speak made his face hurt.

He knew there was a word, but the pain kept him from grasping it.

Then it ended. He opened his eyes, wincing with discomfort. "It hurt," he told the man, "and I couldn't get the word for it."

"It was sunburn," the old man told him.

"It hurt a *lot*," Jonas said, "but I'm glad you gave it to me. It was interesting. And now I understand better, what it meant, that there would be pain."

The man didn't respond. He sat silently for a second. Finally he said, "Get up, now. It's time for you to go home."

They both walked to the center of the room. Jonas put his tunic back on. "Goodbye, sir," he said. "Thank you for my first day."

The old man nodded to him. He looked drained, and a little sad.

"Sir?" Jonas said shyly.

"Yes? Do you have a question?"

"It's just that I don't know your name. I thought you were The Receiver, but you say that now *I'm* The Receiver. So I don't know what to call you."

The man had sat back down in the comfortable upholstered chair. He moved his shoulders around as if to ease away an aching sensation. He seemed terribly weary.

"Call me The Giver," he told Jonas.

Chapter 12

"You slept soundly, Jonas?" his mother asked at the morning meal. "No dreams?"

Jonas simply smiled and nodded, not ready to lie, not willing to tell the truth. "I slept very soundly," he said.

"I wish this one would," his father said, leaning down from his chair to touch Gabriel's waving fist. The basket was on the floor beside him; in its corner, beside Gabriel's head, the stuffed hippo sat staring with its blank eyes.

"So do I," Mother said, rolling her eyes. "He's so fretful at night."

Jonas had not heard the newchild during the night because as always, he *had* slept soundly. But it was not true that he had no dreams.

Again and again, as he slept, he had slid down that snow-covered hill. Always, in the dream, it seemed as if there were a destination: a *something*—he could not grasp what—that lay beyond the place where the thickness of snow brought the sled to a stop.

He was left, upon awakening, with the feeling that he wanted, even somehow needed, to reach the something that waited in the distance. The feeling that it was good. That it was welcoming. That it was significant.

But he did not know how to get there.

He tried to shed the leftover dream, gathering his schoolwork and preparing for the day.

School seemed a little different today. The classes were the same: language and communications; commerce and industry; science and technology; civil procedures and government. But during the breaks for recreation periods and the midday meal, the other new Twelves were abuzz with descriptions of their first day of training. All of them talked at once, interrupting each other, hastily making the required apology for interrupting, then forgetting again in the excitement of describing the new experiences.

Jonas listened. He was very aware of his own admonition not to discuss his training. But it would have been impossible, anyway. There was no way to describe to his friends what he had experienced there in the Annex room. How could you describe a sled without describing a hill and snow; and how could you describe a hill and snow to someone who had never felt height or wind or that feathery, magical cold?

Even trained for years as they all had been in precision of language, what words could you use which would give another the experience of sunshine?

So it was easy for Jonas to be still and to listen.

After school hours he rode again beside Fiona to the House of the Old.

"I looked for you yesterday," she told him, "so we could ride home together. Your bike was still there, and I waited for a little while. But it was getting late, so I went on home."

"I apologize for making you wait," Jonas said.

"I accept your apology," she replied automatically.

"I stayed a little longer than I expected," Jonas explained.

She pedaled forward silently, and he knew that she expected him to tell her why. She expected him to describe his first day of training. But to ask would have fallen into the category of rudeness.

"You've been doing so many volunteer hours with

the Old," Jonas said, changing the subject. "There won't be much that you don't already know."

"Oh, there's lots to learn," Fiona replied. "There's administrative work, and the dietary rules, and punishment for disobedience—did you know that they use a discipline wand on the Old, the same as for small children? And there's occupational therapy, and recreational activities, and medications, and—"

They reached the building and braked their bikes.

"I really think I'll like it better than school," Fiona confessed.

"Me too," Jonas agreed, wheeling his bike into its place.

She waited for a second, as if, again, she expected him to go on. Then she looked at her watch, waved, and hurried toward the entrance.

Jonas stood for a moment beside his bike, startled. It had happened again: the thing that he thought of now as "seeing beyond." This time it had been Fiona who had undergone that fleeting indescribable change. As he looked up and toward her going through the door, it happened; she changed. Actually, Jonas thought, trying to recreate it in his mind, it wasn't Fiona in her entirety. It seemed to be just her hair. And just for that flickering instant.

He ran through it in his mind. It was clearly beginning to happen more often. First, the apple a few weeks before. The next time had been the faces in the audience at the Auditorium, just two days ago. Now, today, Fiona's hair.

Frowning, Jonas walked toward the Annex. I will ask the Giver, he decided.

The old man looked up, smiling, when Jonas entered the room. He was already seated beside the bed, and he seemed more energetic today, slightly renewed, and glad to see Jonas.

"Welcome," he said. "We must get started. You're one minute late."

"I apologi—" Jonas began, and then stopped, flustered, remembering there were to be no apologies.

He removed his tunic and went to the bed. "I'm one minute late because something happened," he explained. "And I'd like to ask you about it, if you don't mind."

"You may ask me anything."

Jonas tried to sort it out in his mind so that he could explain it clearly. "I think it's what you call seeing beyond," he said.

The Giver nodded. "Describe it," he said.

Jonas told him about the experience with the apple. Then the moment on the stage, when he had looked out and seen the same phenomenon in the faces of the crowd.

"Then today, just now, outside, it happened with my friend Fiona. She herself didn't change, exactly. But something about her changed for a second. Her hair looked different; but not in its shape, not in its length. I can't quite—" Jonas paused, frustrated by his inability to grasp and describe exactly what *had* occurred.

Finally he simply said, "It changed. I don't know how, or why.

"That's why I was one minute late," he concluded, and looked questioningly at The Giver.

To his surprise, the old man asked him a question which seemed unrelated to the seeing-beyond. "When I gave you the memory yesterday, the first one, the ride on the sled, did you look around?"

Jonas nodded. "Yes," he said, "but the stuff—I mean the snow—in the air made it hard to see anything."

"Did you look at the sled?"

Jonas thought back. "No. I only felt it under me. I dreamed of it last night, too. But I don't remember *seeing* the sled in my dream, either. Just feeling it."

The Giver seemed to be thinking.

"When I was observing you, before the selection, I perceived that you probably had the capacity, and what you describe confirms that. It happened somewhat differently to me," The Giver told him. "When I was just your age—about to become the new Receiver—I began to experience it, though it took a different form. With me it was . . . well, I won't describe that now, you wouldn't understand it yet.

"But I think I can guess how it's happening with you. Let me just make a little test, to confirm my guess. Lie down."

Jonas lay on the bed again with his hands at his sides. He felt comfortable here now. He closed his eyes and waited for the familiar feel of The Giver's hands on his back.

But it didn't come. Instead, The Giver instructed him, "Call back the memory of the ride on the sled. Just the *beginning* of it, where you're at the top of the hill, before the slide starts. And this time, look down at the sled."

Jonas was puzzled. He opened his eyes. "Excuse me," he asked politely, "but don't *you* have to give me the memory?"

"It's your memory, now. It's not mine to experience any longer. I gave it away."

"But how can I call it back?"

"You can remember last year, or the year that you were a Seven, or a Five, can't you?"

"Of course."

"It's much the same. Everyone in the community

has one-generation memories like those. But now you will be able to go back farther. Try. Just concentrate."

Jonas closed his eyes again. He took a deep breath and sought the sled and the hill and the snow in his consciousness.

There they were, with no effort. He was again sitting in that whirling world of snowflakes, atop the hill.

Jonas grinned with delight, and blew his own steamy breath into view. Then, as he had been instructed, he looked down. He saw his own hands, furred again with snow, holding the rope. He saw his legs, and moved them aside for a glimpse of the sled beneath.

Dumbfounded, he stared at it. This time it was not a fleeting impression. This time the sled had—and continued to have, as he blinked, and stared at it again—that same mysterious quality that the apple had had so briefly. And Fiona's hair. The sled did not change. It simply was—whatever the thing was.

Jonas opened his eyes and was still on the bed. The Giver was watching him curiously.

"Yes," Jonas said slowly. "I saw it, in the sled."

"Let me try one more thing. Look over there, to the bookcase. Do you see the very top row of books, the ones behind the table, on the top shelf?"

Jonas sought them with his eyes. He stared at them, and they changed. But the change was fleeting. It slipped away the next instant.

"It happened," Jonas said. "It happened to the books, but it went away again."

"I'm right, then," The Giver said. "You're beginning to see the color red."

"The what?"

The Giver sighed. "How to explain this? Once,

back in the time of the memories, everything had a shape and size, the way things still do, but they also had a quality called *color.*

"There were a lot of colors, and one of them was called red. That's the one you are starting to see. Your friend Fiona has red hair—quite distinctive, actually; I've noticed it before. When you mentioned Fiona's hair, it was the clue that told me you were probably beginning to see the color red."

"And the faces of people? The ones I saw at the Ceremony?"

The Giver shook his head. "No, flesh isn't red. But it has red tones in it. There was a time, actually— you'll see this in the memories later—when flesh was many different colors. That was before we went to Sameness. Today flesh is all the same, and what you saw was the red tones. Probably when you saw the faces take on color it wasn't as deep or vibrant as the apple, or your friend's hair."

The Giver chuckled, suddenly. "We've never completely mastered Sameness. I suppose the genetic scientists are still hard at work trying to work the kinks out. Hair like Fiona's must drive them crazy."

Jonas listened, trying hard to comprehend. "And the sled?" he said. "It had that same thing: the color red. But it didn't *change,* Giver. It just *was.*"

"Because it's a memory from the time when color *was.*"

"It was so—oh, I wish language were more precise! The red was so beautiful!"

The Giver nodded. "It is."

"Do you see it all the time?"

"I see all of them. All the colors."

"Will I?"

"Of course. When you receive the memories. You have the capacity to see beyond. You'll gain wisdom, then, along with colors. And lots more."

Jonas wasn't interested, just then, in wisdom. It was the colors that fascinated him. "Why can't everyone see them? Why did colors disappear?"

The Giver shrugged. "Our people made that choice, the choice to go to Sameness. Before my time, before the previous time, back and back and back. We relinquished color when we relinquished sunshine and did away with differences." He thought for a moment. "We gained control of many things. But we had to let go of others."

"We shouldn't have!" Jonas said fiercely.

The Giver looked startled at the certainty of Jonas's reaction. Then he smiled wryly. "You've come very quickly to that conclusion," he said. "It took me many years. Maybe your wisdom will come much more quickly than mine."

He glanced at the wall clock "Lie back down, now. We have so much to do."

"Giver," Jonas asked as he arranged himself again on the bed, "how did it happen to you when you were becoming The Receiver? You said that the seeing-beyond happened to you, but not the same way."

The hands came to his back. "Another day," The Giver said gently. "I'll tell you another day. Now we must work. And I've thought of a way to help you with the concept of color.

"Close your eyes and be still, now. I'm going to give you a memory of a rainbow."

Chapter 13

Days went by, and weeks. Jonas learned, through the memories, the names of colors; and now he began to see them all, in his ordinary life (though he knew it was ordinary no longer, and would never be again). But they didn't last. There would be a glimpse of green—the landscaped lawn around the Central Plaza; a bush on the riverbank. The bright orange of pumpkins being trucked in from the agricultural fields beyond the community boundary—seen in an instant, the flash of brilliant color, but gone again, returning to their flat and hueless shade.

The Giver told him that it would be a very long time before he had the colors to keep.

"But I want them!" Jonas said angrily. "It isn't fair that nothing has color!"

"Not fair?" The Giver looked at Jonas curiously. "Explain what you mean."

"Well . . . " Jonas had to stop and think it through. "If everything's the same, then there aren't any choices! I want to wake up in the morning and *decide* things! A blue tunic, or a red one?"

He looked down at himself, at the colorless fabric of his clothing. "But it's all the same, always."

Then he laughed a little. "I know it's not important, what you wear. It doesn't matter. But—"

"It's the choosing that's important, isn't it?" The Giver asked him.

Jonas nodded. "My little brother—" he began, and then corrected himself. "No, that's inaccurate. He's not my brother, not really. But this newchild that my family takes care of—his name's Gabriel?"

"Yes, I know about Gabriel."

"Well, he's right at the age where he's learning so much. He grabs toys when we hold them in front of him—my father says he's learning small-muscle control. And he's really cute."

The Giver nodded.

"But now that I can see colors, at least sometimes, I was just thinking: what if we could hold up things that were bright red, or bright yellow, and he could *choose?* Instead of the Sameness."

"He might make wrong choices."

"Oh." Jonas was silent for a minute. "Oh, I see what you mean. It wouldn't matter for a newchild's toy. But later it *does* matter, doesn't it? We don't dare to let people make choices of their own."

"Not safe?" The Giver suggested.

"Definitely not safe," Jonas said with certainty. "What if they were allowed to choose their own mate? And chose *wrong?*

"Or what if," he went on, almost laughing at the absurdity, "they chose their own *jobs?*"

"Frightening, isn't it?" The Giver said.

Jonas chuckled. "Very frightening. I can't even imagine it. We really have to protect people from wrong choices."

"It's safer."

"Yes," Jonas agreed. "Much safer."

But when the conversation turned to other things, Jonas was left, still, with a feeling of frustration that he didn't understand.

He found that he was often angry, now: irrationally angry at his groupmates, that they were satisfied with their lives which had none of the vibrance his own was taking on. And he was angry at himself, that he could not change that for them.

He tried. Without asking permission from The

Giver, because he feared—or knew—that it would be denied, he tried to give his new awareness to his friends.

"Asher," Jonas said one morning, "look at those flowers very carefully." They were standing beside a bed of geraniums planted near the Hall of Open Records. He put his hands on Asher's shoulders, and concentrated on the red of the petals, trying to hold it as long as he could, and trying at the same time to transmit the awareness of red to his friend.

"What's the matter?" Asher asked uneasily. "Is something wrong?" He moved away from Jonas's hands. It was extremely rude for one citizen to touch another outside of family units.

"No, nothing. I thought for a minute that they were wilting, and we should let the Gardening Crew know they needed more watering." Jonas sighed, and turned away.

One evening he came home from his training weighted with new knowledge. The Giver had chosen a startling and disturbing memory that day. Under the touch of his hands, Jonas had found himself suddenly in a place that was completely alien: hot and windswept under a vast blue sky. There were tufts of sparse grass, a few bushes and rocks, and nearby he could see an area of thick vegetation: broad, low trees outlined against the sky. He could hear noises: the sharp crack of weapons— he perceived the word *guns*—and then shouts, and an immense crashing thud as something fell, tearing branches from the trees.

He heard voices calling to one another. Peering from the place where he stood hidden behind some shrubbery, he was reminded of what The Giver had told him, that there had been a time when flesh had different colors. Two of these men had dark brown skin; the others were light. Going closer, he watched them hack the tusks from a motionless elephant on the ground and haul them away, spattered with blood. He felt himself overwhelmed with a new perception of the color he knew as red.

Then the men were gone, speeding toward the horizon in a vehicle that spit pebbles from its whirling tires. One hit his forehead and stung him there. But the memory continued, though Jonas ached now for it to end.

Now he saw another elephant emerge from the place where it had stood hidden in the trees. Very slowly it walked to the mutilated body and looked down. With its sinuous trunk it stroked the huge corpse; then it reached up, broke some leafy branches with a snap, and draped them over the mass of torn thick flesh.

Finally it tilted its massive head, raised its trunk, and roared into the empty landscape. Jonas had never heard such a sound. It was a sound of rage and grief and it seemed never to end.

He could still hear it when he opened his eyes and lay anguished on the bed where he received the memories. It continued to roar into his consciousness as he pedaled slowly home.

"Lily," he asked that evening when his sister took her comfort object, the stuffed elephant, from the shelf, "did you know that once there really were elephants? Live ones?"

She glanced down at the ragged comfort object and grinned. "Right," she said, skeptically. "Sure, Jonas."

Jonas went and sat beside them while his father untied Lily's hair ribbons and combed her hair. He placed one hand on each of their shoulders. With all of his being he tried to give each of them a piece of the memory: not of the tortured cry of the elephant, but of the *being* of the elephant, of the towering, immense creature and the meticulous touch with which it had tended its friend at the end.

But his father had continued to comb Lily's long hair, and Lily, impatient, had finally wiggled under her brother's touch. "Jonas," she said, "you're hurting me with your hand."

"I apologize for hurting you, Lily," Jonas mumbled, and took his hand away.

"'Ccept your apology," Lily responded indifferently, stroking the lifeless elephant.

"Giver," Jonas asked once, as they prepared for the day's work, "don't you have a spouse? Aren't you allowed to apply for one?" Although he was exempted from the rules against rudeness, he was aware that this was a rude question. But The Giver had encouraged all of his questions, not seeming to be embarrassed or offended by even the most personal.

The Giver chuckled. "No, there's no rule against it. And I did have a spouse. You're forgetting how old I am, Jonas. My former spouse lives now with the Childless Adults."

"Oh, of course." Jonas *had* forgotten The Giver's obvious age. When adults of the community became older, their lives became different. They were no longer needed to create family units. Jonas's own parents, when he and Lily were grown, would go to live with the Childless Adults.

"You'll be able to apply for a spouse, Jonas, if you want to. I'll warn you, though, that it will be difficult. Your living arrangements will have to be different from those of most family units, because the books are forbidden to citizens. You and I are the only ones with access to the books."

Jonas glanced around at the astonishing array of volumes. From time to time, now, he could see their colors. With their hours together, his and The Giver's, consumed by conversation and by the transmission of memories, Jonas had not yet opened any of the books. But he read the titles here and there, and knew that they contained all of the knowledge of centuries, and that one day they would belong to him.

"So if I have a spouse, and maybe children, I will have to hide the books from them?"

The Giver nodded. "I wasn't permitted to share the books with my spouse, that's correct. And there are other difficulties, too. You remember the rule that says the new Receiver can't talk about his training?"

Jonas nodded. Of course he remembered. It had turned out, by far, to be the most frustrating of the rules he was required to obey.

"When you become the official Receiver, when we're finished here, you'll be given a whole new set of rules. Those are the rules that I obey. And it won't surprise you that I am forbidden to talk about my work to anyone except the new Receiver. That's you, of course.

"So there will be a whole part of your life which you won't be able to share with a family. It's hard, Jonas. It was hard for me.

"You do understand, don't you, that this *is* my life? The memories?"

Jonas nodded again, but he was puzzled. Didn't life consist of the things you did each day? There wasn't anything else, really. "I've seen you taking walks," he said.

The Giver sighed. "I walk. I eat at mealtime. And

when I am called by the Committee of Elders, I appear before them, to give them counsel and advice."

"Do you advise them often?" Jonas was a little frightened at the thought that one day he would be the one to advise the ruling body.

But The Giver said no. "Rarely. Only when they are faced with something that they have not experienced before. Then they call upon me to use the memories and advise them. But it very seldom happens. Sometimes I wish they'd ask for my wisdom more often—there are so many things I could tell them; things I wish they would change. But they don't want change. Life here is so orderly, so predictable—so painless. It's what they've chosen."

"I don't know why they even *need* a Receiver, then, if they never call upon him," Jonas commented.

"They need me. And you," The Giver said, but didn't explain. "They were reminded of that ten years ago."

"What happened ten years ago?" Jonas asked. "Oh, I know. You tried to train a successor and it failed. Why? Why did that remind them?"

The Giver smiled grimly. "When the new Receiver failed, the memories that she had received were released. They didn't come back to me. They went . . . "

He paused, and seemed to be struggling with the concept. "I don't know, exactly. They went to the place where memories once existed before Receivers were created. Someplace out *there*—" He gestured vaguely with his arm. "And then the people had access to them. Apparently that's the way it was, once. Everyone had access to memories.

"It was chaos," he said. "They really suffered for a while. Finally it subsided as the memories were assimilated. But it certainly made them aware of how they need a Receiver to contain all that pain. And knowledge."

"But you have to suffer like that all the time," Jonas pointed out.

The Giver nodded. "And you will. It's my life. It will be yours."

Jonas thought about it, about what it would be like for him. "Along with walking and eating and—" He looked around the walls of books. "Reading? That's it?"

The Giver shook his head. "Those are simply the things that I *do*. My *life* is here."

"In this room?"

The Giver shook his head. He put his hands on his own face, to his chest. "No. Here, in my being. Where the memories are."

"My instructors in science and technology have taught us about how the brain works," Jonas told him eagerly. "It's full of electrical impulses. It's like a computer. If you stimulate one part of the brain with an electrode, it—" He stopped talking. He could see an odd look on The Giver's face.

"They know nothing," The Giver said bitterly.

Jonas was shocked. Since the first day in the Annex room, they had together disregarded the rules about rudeness, and Jonas felt comfortable with that now. But this was different, and far beyond rude. This was a terrible accusation. What if someone had heard?

He glanced quickly at the wall speaker, terrified that the committee might be listening as they could at any time. But, as always during their sessions together, the switch had been turned to OFF.

"Nothing?" Jonas whispered nervously. "But my instructors—"

The Giver flicked his hand as if brushing something aside. "Oh, your instructors are well trained. They know their scientific facts. *Everyone* is well trained for his job.

"It's just that . . . without the memories it's all meaningless. They gave that burden to me. And to the previous Receiver. And to the one before him."

"And back and back and back," Jonas said, knowing the phrase that always came.

The Giver smiled, though his smile was oddly harsh. "That's right. And next it will be you. A great honor."

"Yes, sir. They told me that at the Ceremony. The very highest honor."

Some afternoons The Giver sent him away without training. Jonas knew, on days when he arrived to find The Giver hunched over, rocking his body slightly back and forth, his face pale, that he would be sent away.

"Go," The Giver would tell him tensely. "I'm in pain today. Come back tomorrow."

On those days, worried and disappointed, Jonas would walk alone beside the river. The paths were empty of people except for the few Delivery Crews and Landscape Workers here and there. Small children were all at the Childcare Center after school, and the older ones busy with volunteer hours or training.

By himself, he tested his own developing memory. He watched the landscape for glimpses of the green that he knew was embedded in the shrubbery; when it came flickering into his consciousness, he focused upon it, keeping it there, darkening it, holding it in his vision as long as possible until his head hurt and he let it fade away.

He stared at the flat, colorless sky, bringing blue from it, and remembered sunshine until finally, for an instant, he could feel warmth.

He stood at the foot of the bridge that spanned the river, the bridge that citizens were allowed to cross only on official business. Jonas had crossed it on school trips, visiting the outlying communities, and he knew that the land beyond the bridge was much the same, flat and well ordered, with fields for agriculture. The other communities he had seen on visits were essentially the same as his own, the only differences were slightly altered styles of dwellings, slightly different schedules in the schools.

He wondered what lay in the far distance where he had never gone. The land didn't *end* beyond those nearby communities. Were there *hills* Elsewhere? Were there vast wind-torn areas like the place he had seen in memory, the place where the elephant died?

"Giver," he asked one afternoon following a day when he had been sent away, "what causes you pain?"

When The Giver was silent, Jonas continued. "The Chief Elder told me, at the beginning, that the receiving of memory causes terrible pain. And you described for me that the failure of the last new Receiver released painful memories to the community.

"But I haven't suffered, Giver. Not really." Jonas smiled. "Oh, I remember the sunburn you gave me on the very first day. But that wasn't so terrible. What is it that makes you suffer so much? If you gave some of it to me, maybe your pain would be less."

The Giver nodded. "Lie down," he said. "It's time, I suppose. I can't shield you forever. You'll have to take it all on eventually.

"Let me think," he went on, when Jonas was on the bed, waiting, a little fearful.

"All right," The Giver said after a moment, "I've decided. We'll start with something familiar. Let's go once again to a hill, and a sled."

He placed his hands on Jonas's back.

Chapter 14

It was much the same, this memory, though the hill seemed to be a different one, steeper, and the snow was not falling as thickly as it had before.

It was colder, also, Jonas perceived. He could see, as he sat waiting at the top of the hill, that the snow beneath the sled was not thick and soft as it had been before, but hard, and coated with bluish ice.

The sled moved forward, and Jonas grinned with delight, looking forward to the breathtaking slide down through the invigorating air.

But the runners, this time, couldn't slice through the frozen expanse as they had on the other, snow-cushioned hill. They skittered sideways and the sled gathered speed. Jonas pulled at the rope, trying to steer, but the steepness and speed took control from his hands and he was no longer enjoying the feeling of freedom but instead, terrified, was at the mercy of the wild acceleration downward over the ice.

Sideways, spinning, the sled hit a bump in the hill and Jonas was jarred loose and thrown violently into the air. He fell with his leg twisted under him, and could hear the crack of bone. His face scraped along jagged edges of ice and when he came, at last, to a stop, he lay shocked and still,. feeling nothing at first but fear.

Then, the first wave of pain. He gasped. It was as if a hatchet lay lodged in his leg, slicing through each nerve with a hot blade. In his agony he perceived the word "fire" and felt flames licking at the torn bone and flesh. He tried to move, and could not. The pain grew.

He screamed. There was no answer.

Sobbing, he turned his head and vomited onto the frozen snow. Blood dripped from his face into the vomit.

"Nooooo!" he cried, and the sound disappeared into the empty landscape, into the wind.

Then, suddenly, he was in the Annex room again, writhing on the bed. His face was wet with tears.

Able to move now, he rocked his own body back and forth, breathing deeply to release the remembered pain.

He sat, and looked at his own leg, where it lay straight on the bed, unbroken. The brutal slice of pain was gone. But the leg ached horribly, still, and his face felt raw.

"May I have relief-of-pain, please?" he begged. It was always provided in his everyday life for the bruises and wounds, for a mashed finger, a stomach ache, a skinned knee from a fall from a bike. There was always a daub of anesthetic ointment, or a pill; or in severe instances, an injection that brought complete and instantaneous deliverance.

But The Giver said no, and looked away.

Limping, Jonas walked home, pushing his bicycle, that evening. The sunburn pain had been so small, in comparison, and had not stayed with him. But this ache lingered.

It was not unendurable, as the pain on the hill had been. Jonas tried to be brave. He remembered that the Chief Elder had said he was brave.

"Is something wrong, Jonas?" his father asked at the evening meal. "You're so quiet tonight. Aren't you feeling well? Would you like some medication?"

But Jonas remembered the rules. No medication for anything related to his training.

And no discussion of his training. At the time for

sharing of feelings, he simply said that he felt tired, that his school lessons had been unusually demanding that day.

He went to his sleepingroom early, and from behind the closed door he could hear his parents and sister laughing as they gave Gabriel his evening bath.

They have never known pain, he thought. The realization made him feel desperately lonely, and he rubbed his throbbing leg. He eventually slept. Again and again he dreamed of the anguish and the isolation on the forsaken hill.

The daily training continued, and now it always included pain. The agony of the fractured leg began to seem no more than a mild discomfort as The Giver led Jonas firmly, little by little, into the deep and terrible suffering of the past. Each time, in his kindness, The Giver ended the afternoon with a color-filled memory of pleasure: a brisk sail on a blue-green lake, a meadow dotted with yellow wildflowers; an orange sunset behind mountains.

It was not enough to assuage the pain that Jonas was beginning, now, to know.

"*Why?*" Jonas asked him after he had received a torturous memory in which he had been neglected and unfed; the hunger had caused excruciating spasms in his empty, distended stomach. He lay on the bed, aching. "Why do you and I have to hold these memories?"

"It gives us wisdom," The Giver replied. "Without wisdom I could not fulfill my function of advising the Committee of Elders when they call upon me."

"But what wisdom do you get from hunger?" Jonas groaned. His stomach still hurt, though the memory had ended.

"Some years ago," The Giver told him, "before

your birth, a lot of citizens petitioned the Committee of Elders. They wanted to increase the rate of births. They wanted each Birthmother to be assigned four births instead of three, so that the population would increase and there would be more Laborers available."

Jonas nodded, listening. "That makes sense."

"The idea was that certain family units could accommodate an additional child."

Jonas nodded again. "Mine could," he pointed out. "We have Gabriel this year, and it's fun, having a third child."

"The Committee of Elders sought my advice," The Giver said. "It made sense to them, too, but it was a new idea, and they came to me for wisdom."

"And you used your memories?"

The Giver said yes. "And the strongest memory that came was hunger. It came from many generations back. *Centuries* back. The population had gotten so big that hunger was everywhere. Excruciating hunger and starvation. It was followed by warfare."

"Warfare?" It was a concept Jonas did not know. But hunger was familiar to him now. Unconsciously he rubbed his own abdomen, recalling the pain of its unfulfilled needs. "So you described that to them?"

"They don't want to hear about pain. They just seek the advice. I simply advised them against increasing the population."

"But you said that that was before my birth. They hardly ever come to you for advice. Only when they— what was it you said? When they have a problem they've never faced before. When did it happen last?"

"Do you remember the day when the plane flew over the community?"

"Yes. I was scared."

"So were they. They prepared to shoot it down. But they sought my advice. I told them to wait."

"But how did you know? How did you know the Pilot was lost?"

"I didn't. I used my wisdom, from the memories. I knew that there had been times in the past—terrible times—when people had destroyed others in haste, in fear, and had brought about their own destruction."

Jonas realized something. "That means," he said slowly, "that you have memories of destruction. And you have to give them to me, too, because I have to get the wisdom."

The Giver nodded.

"But it will hurt," Jonas said. It wasn't a question.

"It will hurt terribly," The Giver agreed.

"But why can't *everyone* have the memories? I think it would seem a little easier if the memories were shared. You and I wouldn't have to bear so much by ourselves, if everybody took a part."

The Giver sighed. "You're right," he said. "But then everyone would be burdened and pained. They don't want that. And that's the real reason The Receiver is so vital to them, and so honored. They selected me—and you—to lift that burden from themselves."

"Why did they decide that?" Jonas asked angrily. "It wasn't fair. Let's change it!"

"How do you suggest we do that? I've never been able to think of a way, and I'm supposed to be the one with all the wisdom."

"But there are two of us now," Jonas said eagerly. "*Together* we can think of something!"

The Giver watched him with a wry smile.

"Why can't we just apply for a change of rules?" Jonas suggested.

The Giver laughed; then Jonas, too, chuckled reluctantly.

"The decision was made long before my time or yours," The Giver said, "and before the previous Receiver, and—" He waited.

"Back and back and back." Jonas repeated the familiar phrase. Sometimes it had seemed humorous to him. Sometimes it had seemed meaningful and important.

Now it was ominous. It meant, he knew, that nothing could be changed.

The newchild, Gabriel, was growing, and successfully passed the tests of maturity that the Nurturers gave each month; he could sit alone, now, could reach for and grasp small play objects, and he had six teeth. During the daytime hours, Father reported, he was cheerful and seemed of normal intelligence. But he remained fretful at night, whimpering often, needing frequent attention.

"After all this extra time I've put in with him," Father said one evening after Gabriel had been bathed and was lying, for the moment, hugging his hippo placidly in the small crib that had replaced the basket, "I hope they're not going to decide to release him."

"Maybe it would be for the best," Mother suggested. "I know you don't mind getting up with him at night. But the lack of sleep is awfully hard for me."

"If they release Gabriel, can we get another newchild as a visitor?" asked Lily. She was kneeling beside the crib, making funny faces at the little one, who was smiling back at her.

Jonas's mother rolled her eyes in dismay.

"No," Father said, smiling. He ruffled Lily's hair.

"It's very rare, anyway, that a newchild's status is as uncertain as Gabriel's. It probably won't happen again, for a long time.

"Anyway," he sighed, "they won't make the decision for a while. Right now we're all preparing for a release we'll probably have to make very soon. There's a Birthmother who's expecting twin males next month."

"Oh, dear," Mother said, shaking her head. "If they're identical, I hope you're not the one assigned—"

"I am. I'm next on the list. I'll have to select the one to be nurtured, and the one to be released. It's usually not hard, though. Usually it's just a matter of birthweight. We release the smaller of the two."

Jonas, listening, thought suddenly about the bridge and how, standing there, he had wondered what lay Elsewhere. Was there someone there, waiting, who would receive the tiny released twin? Would it grow up Elsewhere, not knowing, ever, that in this community lived a being who looked exactly the same?

For a moment he felt a tiny, fluttering hope that he knew was quite foolish. He hoped that it would be Larissa, waiting. Larissa, the old woman he had bathed. He remembered her sparkling eyes, her soft voice, her low chuckle. Fiona had told him recently that Larissa had been released at a wonderful ceremony.

But he knew that the Old were not given children to raise. Larissa's life Elsewhere would be quiet and serene as befit the Old; she would not welcome the responsibility of nurturing a newchild who needed feeding and care, and would likely cry at night.

"Mother? Father?" he said, the idea coming to him unexpectedly, "why don't we put Gabriel's crib in my room tonight? I know how to feed and comfort him, and it would let you and Father get some sleep."

Father looked doubtful. "You sleep so soundly, Jonas. What if his restlessness didn't wake you?"

It was Lily who answered that. "If no one goes to tend Gabriel," she pointed out, "he gets very loud. He'd wake *all* of us, if Jonas slept through it."

Father laughed. "You're right, Lily-billy. All right, Jonas, let's try it, just for tonight. I'll take the night off and we'll let Mother get some sleep, too."

Gabriel slept soundly for the earliest part of the night. Jonas, in his bed, lay awake for a while; from time to time he raised himself on one elbow, looking over at the crib. The newchild was on his stomach, his arms relaxed beside his head, his eyes closed, and his breathing regular and undisturbed. Finally Jonas slept too.

Then, as the middle hours of the night approached, the noise of Gabe's restlessness woke Jonas. The newchild was turning under his cover, flailing his arms, and beginning to whimper.

Jonas rose and went to him. Gently he patted Gabriel's back. Sometimes that was all it took to lull him back to sleep. But the newchild still squirmed fretfully under his hand.

Still patting rhythmically, Jonas began to remember the wonderful sail that The Giver had given him not long before: a bright, breezy day on a clear turquoise lake, and above him the white sail of the boat billowing as he moved along in the brisk wind.

He was not aware of giving the memory; but suddenly he realized that it was becoming dimmer, that it was sliding through his hand into the being of the newchild. Gabriel became quiet. Startled, Jonas pulled back what was left of the memory with a burst of will. He removed his hand from the little back and stood quietly beside the crib.

To himself, he called the memory of the sail forward again. It was still there, but the sky was less blue, the gentle motion of the boat slower, the water of the lake more murky and clouded. He kept it for a while, soothing his own nervousness at what had occurred, then let it go and returned to his bed.

Once more, toward dawn, the newchild woke and cried out. Again Jonas went to him. This time he quite deliberately placed his hand firmly on Gabriel's back, and released the rest of the calming day on the lake. Again Gabriel slept.

But now Jonas lay awake, thinking. He no longer had any more than a wisp of the memory, and he felt a small lack where it had been. He could ask The Giver for another sail, he knew. A sail perhaps on ocean, next time, for Jonas had a memory of ocean, now, and knew what it was; he knew that there were sailboats there, too, in memories yet to be acquired.

He wondered, though, if he should confess to The Giver that he had given a memory away. He was not yet qualified to be a Giver himself; nor had Gabriel been selected to be a Receiver.

That he had this power frightened him. He decided not to tell.

Chapter 15

Jonas entered the Annex room and realized immediately that it was a day when he would be sent away. The Giver was rigid in his chair, his face in his hands.

"I'll come back tomorrow, sir," he said quickly. Then he hesitated. "Unless maybe there's something I can do to help."

The Giver looked up at him, his face contorted with suffering. "Please," he gasped, "take some of the pain."

Jonas helped him to his chair at the side of the bed. Then he quickly removed his tunic and lay face down. "Put your hands on me," he directed, aware that in such anguish The Giver might need reminding.

The hands came, and the pain came with them and through them. Jonas braced himself and entered the memory which was torturing The Giver.

He was in a confused, noisy, foul-smelling place. It was daylight, early morning, and the air was thick with smoke that hung, yellow and brown, above the ground. Around him, everywhere, far across the expanse of what seemed to be a field, lay groaning men. A wild-eyed horse, its bridle torn and dangling, trotted frantically through the mounds of men, tossing its head, whinnying in panic. It stumbled, finally, then fell, and did not rise.

Jonas heard a voice next to him. "Water," the voice said in a parched, croaking whisper.

He turned his head toward the voice and looked into the half-closed eyes of a boy who seemed not much older than himself. Dirt streaked the boy's face and his matted blond hair. He lay sprawled, his gray uniform glistening with wet, fresh blood.

The colors of the carnage were grotesquely bright: the crimson wetness on the rough and dusty fabric, the ripped shreds of grass, startlingly green, in the boy's yellow hair.

The boy stared at him. "Water," he begged again. When he spoke, a new spurt of blood drenched the coarse cloth across his chest and sleeve.

One of Jonas's arms was immobilized with pain, and he could see through his own torn sleeve something that looked like ragged flesh and splintery bone. He tried his remaining arm and felt it move. Slowly he reached to his side, felt the metal container there, and removed its cap, stopping the small motion of his hand now and then to wait for the surging pain to ease. Finally, when the container was open, he extended his arm slowly across the blood-soaked earth, inch by inch, and held it to the lips of the boy. Water trickled into the imploring mouth and down the grimy chin.

The boy sighed. His head fell back, his lower jaw dropping as if he had been surprised by something. A dull blankness slid slowly across his eyes. He was silent.

But the noise continued all around: the cries of the wounded men, the cries begging for water and for Mother and for death. Horses lying on the ground shrieked, raised their heads, and stabbed randomly toward the sky with their hooves.

From the distance, Jonas could hear the thud of cannons. Overwhelmed by pain, he lay there in the fearsome stench for hours, listened to the men and animals die, and learned what warfare meant.

Finally, when he knew that he could bear it no

longer and would welcome death himself, he opened his eyes and was once again on the bed.

The Giver looked away, as if he could not bear to see what he had done to Jonas. "Forgive me," he said.

Chapter 16

Jonas did not want to go back. He didn't want the memories, didn't want the honor, didn't want the wisdom, didn't want the pain. He wanted his childhood again, his scraped knees and ball games. He sat in his dwelling alone, watching through the window, seeing children at play, citizens bicycling home from uneventful days at work, ordinary lives free of anguish because he had been selected, as others before him had, to bear their burden.

But the choice was not his. He returned each day to the Annex room.

The Giver was gentle with him for many days following the terrible shared memory of war.

"There are so many good memories," The Giver reminded Jonas. And it was true. By now Jonas had experienced countless bits of happiness, things he had never known of before.

He had seen a birthday party, with one child singled out and celebrated on his day, so that now he understood the joy of being an individual, special and unique and proud.

He had visited museums, and seen paintings filled with all the colors he could now recognize and name.

In one ecstatic memory he had ridden a gleaming brown horse across a field that smelled of damp grass, and had dismounted beside a small stream from which both he and the horse drank cold, clear water. Now he understood about animals; and in the moment that the horse turned from the stream and nudged Jonas's shoulder affectionately with its head, he perceived the bonds between animal and human.

He had walked through woods, and sat at night beside a campfire. Although he had through the memories learned about the pain of loss and loneliness, now he gained, too, an understanding of solitude and its joy.

"What is your favorite?" Jonas asked The Giver. "You don't have to give it away yet," he added quickly. "Just tell me about it, so I can look forward to it, because I'll have to receive it when your job is done."

The Giver smiled. "Lie down," he said. "I'm happy to give it to you."

Jonas felt the joy of it as soon as the memory began. Sometimes it took a while for him to get his bearings, to find his place. But this time he fit right in and felt the happiness that pervaded the memory.

He was in a room filled with people, and it was warm, with firelight glowing on a hearth. He could see through a window that outside it was night, and snowing. There were colored lights: red and green and yellow, twinkling from a tree which was, oddly, inside the room. On a table, lighted candles stood in a polished golden holder and cast a soft, flickering glow. He could smell things cooking, and he heard soft laughter. A golden-haired dog lay sleeping on the floor.

On the floor there were packages wrapped in brightly colored paper and tied with gleaming ribbons. As Jonas watched, a small child began to pick up the packages and pass them around the room: to other children, to adults who were obviously parents, and to an older, quiet couple, man and woman, who sat smiling together on a couch.

While Jonas watched, the people began one by one to untie the ribbons on the packages, to unwrap the bright papers, open the boxes and reveal toys and clothing and books. There were cries of delight. They hugged one another.

The small child went and sat on the lap of the old woman, and she rocked him and rubbed her cheek against his.

Jonas opened his eyes and lay contentedly on the bed, still luxuriating in the warm and comforting memory. It had all been there, all the things he had learned to treasure.

"What did you perceive?" The Giver asked.

"Warmth," Jonas replied, "and happiness. And— let me think. *Family.* That it was a celebration of some sort, a holiday. And something else—I can't quite get the word for it."

"It will come to you."

"Who were the old people? Why were they there?" It had puzzled Jonas, seeing them in the room. The Old of the community did not ever leave their special place, the House of the Old, where they were so well cared for and respected.

"They were called Grandparents."

"Grand parents?"

"Grandparents. It meant parents-of-the-parents, long ago."

"Back and back and back?" Jonas began to laugh. "So actually, there could be parents-of-the-parents-of-the-parents-of-the-parents?"

The Giver laughed, too. "That's right. It's a little like looking at yourself looking in a mirror looking at yourself looking in a mirror."

Jonas frowned. "But my parents must have had parents! I never thought about it before. Who are my parents-of-the-parents? *Where* are they?"

"You could go look in the Hall of Open Records. You'd find the names. But think, son. If you apply for children, then who will be their parents-of-the-parents? Who will be their grandparents?"

"My mother and father, of course."

"And where will they be?"

Jonas thought. "Oh," he said slowly. "When I finish my training and become a full adult, I'll be given my dwelling. And then when Lily does, a few years later, she'll get *her* own dwelling, and maybe a spouse, and children if she applies for them, and then Mother and Father—"

"That's right."

"As long as they're still working and contributing to the community, they'll go and live with the other Childless Adults. And they won't be part of my life anymore.

"And after that, when the time comes, they'll go to the House of the Old," Jonas went on. He was thinking aloud. "And they'll be well cared for, and respected, and when they're released, there will be a celebration."

"Which you won't attend," The Giver pointed out.

"No, of course not, because I won't even know about it. By then I'll be so busy with my own life. And Lily will, too. So our children, if we have them, won't know who their parents-of-parents are, either.

"It seems to work pretty well that way, doesn't it? The way we do it in our community?" Jonas asked. "I just didn't realize there was any other way, until I received that memory."

"It works," The Giver agreed.

Jonas hesitated. "I certainly liked the memory, though. I can see why it's your favorite. I couldn't quite get the word for the whole feeling of it, the feeling that was so strong in the room."

"Love," The Giver told him.

Jonas repeated it. "Love." It was a word and concept new to him.

They were both silent for a minute. Then Jonas said, "Giver?"

"Yes?"

"I feel very foolish saying this. Very, very foolish."

"No need. Nothing is foolish here. Trust the memories and how they make you feel."

"Well," Jonas said, looking at the floor, "I know you don't have the memory anymore, because you gave it to me, so maybe you won't understand this—"

"I will. I am left with a vague wisp of that one; and I have many other memories of families, and holidays, and happiness. Of love."

Jonas blurted out what he was feeling. "I was thinking that . . well, I can see that it wasn't a very practical way to live, with the Old right there in the same place, where maybe they wouldn't be well taken care of, the way they are now, and that we have a better-arranged way of doing things. But anyway, I was thinking, I mean feeling, actually, that it was kind of nice, then. And that I wish we could be that way, and that you could be my grandparent. The family in the memory seemed a little more—" He faltered, not able to find the word he wanted.

"A little more complete," The Giver suggested.

Jonas nodded. "I liked the feeling of love," he confessed. He glanced nervously at the speaker on the wall, reassuring himself that no one was listening. "I wish we still had that," he whispered. "Of course," he added quickly, "I do understand that it wouldn't work very well. And that it's much better to be organized the way we are now. I can see that it was a *dangerous* way to live."

"What do you mean?"

Jonas hesitated. He wasn't certain, really, what he had meant. He could feel that there was *risk* involved, though he wasn't sure how. "Well," he said finally, grasping for an explanation, "they had *fire* right there in that room. There was a fire burning in the fireplace. And there were candles on a table. I can certainly see why those things were outlawed.

"Still," he said slowly, almost to himself, "I did like the light they made. And the warmth."

"Father? Mother?" Jonas asked tentatively after the evening meal. "I have a question I want to ask you."

"What is it, Jonas?" his father asked.

He made himself say the words, though he felt flushed with embarrassment. He had rehearsed them in his mind all the way home from the Annex.

"Do you love me?"

There was an awkward silence for a moment. Then Father gave a little chuckle. "*Jonas.* You, of all people. Precision of language, *please!*"

"What do you mean?" Jonas asked. Amusement was not at all what he had anticipated.

"Your father means that you used a very generalized word, so meaningless that it's become almost obsolete," his mother explained carefully.

Jonas stared at them. Meaningless? He had never before felt anything as meaningful as the memory.

"And of course our community can't function smoothly if people don't use precise language. You could ask, 'Do you enjoy me?' The answer is 'Yes,'" his mother said.

"Or," his father suggested, " 'Do you take pride in my accomplishments?' And the answer is whole-heartedly 'Yes.'"

"Do you understand why it's inappropriate to use a word like 'love'?" Mother asked.

Jonas nodded. "Yes, thank you, I do," he replied slowly.

It was his first lie to his parents.

"Gabriel?" Jonas whispered that night to the newchild. The crib was in his room again. After Gabe had slept soundly in Jonas's room for four nights, his parents had pronounced the experiment a success and Jonas a hero. Gabriel was growing rapidly, now crawling and giggling across the room and pulling himself up to stand. He could be upgraded in the Nurturing Center, Father said happily, now that he slept; he could be officially named and given to his family in December, which was only two months away.

But when he was taken away, he stopped sleeping again, and cried in the night.

So he was back in Jonas's sleepingroom. They would give it a little more time, they decided. Since Gabe seemed to like it in Jonas's room, he would sleep there at night a little longer, until the habit of sound sleep was fully formed. The Nurturers were very optimistic about Gabriel's future.

There was no answer to Jonas's whisper. Gabriel was sound asleep.

"Things could change, Gabe," Jonas went on "Things could be different. I don't know how, but there must be some way for things to be different. There could be colors.

"And grandparents," he added, staring through the dimness toward the ceiling of his sleepingroom. "And everybody would have the memories.

"You know about memories," he whispered, turning toward the crib.

Gabriel's breathing was even and deep. Jonas liked having him there, though he felt guilty about the secret. Each night he gave memories to Gabriel: memories of boat rides and picnics in the sun;

memories of soft rainfall against windowpanes; memories of dancing barefoot on a damp lawn.

"Gabe?"

The newchild stirred slightly in his sleep. Jonas looked over at him.

"There could be love," Jonas whispered.

The next morning, for the first time, Jonas did not take his pill. Something within him, something that had grown there through the memories, told him to throw the pill away.

Chapter 17

Today is declared an unscheduled holiday. Jonas, his parents, and Lily all turned in surprise and looked at the wall speaker from which the announcement had come. It happened so rarely, and was such a treat for the entire community when it did. Adults were exempted from the day's work, children from school and training and volunteer hours. The substitute Laborers, who would be given a different holiday, took over all the necessary tasks: nurturing, food delivery, and care of the Old; and the community was free.

Jonas cheered, and put his homework folder down. He had been about to leave for school. School was less important to him now, and before much more time passed, his formal schooling would end. But still, for Twelves, though they had begun their adult training, there were the endless lists of rules to be memorized and the newest technology to be mastered.

He wished his parents, sister, and Gabe a happy day, and rode down the bicycle path, looking for Asher.

He had not taken the pills, now, for four weeks. The Stirrings had returned, and he felt a little guilty and embarrassed about the pleasurable dreams that came to him as he slept. But he knew he couldn't go back to the world of no feelings that he had lived in so long.

And his new, heightened feelings permeated a greater realm than simply his sleep. Though he knew that his failure to take the pills accounted for some of it, he thought that the feelings came also from the memories. Now he could see all of the colors; and he could *keep* them, too, so that the trees and grass and bushes stayed green in his vision. Gabriel's rosy cheeks stayed pink, even when he slept. And apples were always, always red.

Now, through the memories, he had seen oceans and mountain lakes and streams that gurgled through woods; and now he saw the familiar wide river beside the path differently. He saw all of the light and color and history it contained and carried in its slow-moving water; and he knew that there was an Elsewhere from which it came, and an Elsewhere to which it was going.

On this unexpected, casual holiday he felt happy, as he always had on holidays; but with a deeper happiness than ever before. Thinking, as he always did, about precision of language, Jonas realized that it was a new *depth* of feelings that he was experiencing. Somehow they were not at all the same as the feelings that every evening, in every dwelling, every citizen analyzed with endless talk.

"I felt angry because someone broke the play area rules," Lily had said once, making a fist with her small hand to indicate her fury. Her family—Jonas among them—had talked about the possible reasons for rule-breaking, and the need for understanding and patience, until Lily's fist had relaxed and her anger was gone.

But Lily had not felt anger, Jonas realized now. Shallow impatience and exasperation, that was all Lily had felt. He knew that with certainty because now he knew what anger was. Now he had, in the memories, experienced injustice and cruelty, and he had reacted with rage that welled up so passionately inside him that the thought of discussing it calmly at the evening meal was unthinkable.

"I felt sad today," he had heard his mother say, and they had comforted her.

But now Jonas had experienced real sadness. He had felt grief. He knew that there was no quick comfort for emotions like those.

These were deeper and they did not need to be told. They were *felt*.

Today, he felt happiness.

"Asher!" He spied his friend's bicycle leaning against a tree at the edge of the playing field. Nearby, other bikes were strewn about on the ground. On a holiday the usual rules of order could be disregarded.

He skidded to a stop and dropped his own bike beside the others. "Hey, Ash!" he shouted, looking around. There seemed to be no one in the play area. "Where are you?"

"Psssheeewwww!" A child's voice, coming from behind a nearby bush, made the sound. "Pow! Pow! Pow!"

A female Eleven named Tanya staggered forward from where she had been hiding. Dramatically she clutched her stomach and stumbled about in a zig-zag pattern, groaning. "You got me," she called, and fell to the ground, grinning.

"Blam!"

Jonas, standing on the side of the playing field, recognized Asher's voice. He saw his friend, aiming an imaginary weapon in his hand, dart from behind one tree to another. "Blam! You're in my line of ambush, Jonas! Watch out!"

Jonas stepped back. He moved behind Asher's bike and knelt so that he was out of sight. It was a game he had often played with the other children, a game of good guys and bad guys, a harmless pastime that used up their contained energy and ended only when they all lay posed in freakish postures on the ground.

He had never recognized it before as a game of war.

"Attack!" The shout came from behind the small Storehouse where play equipment was kept. Three children dashed forward, their imaginary weapons in firing position.

From the opposite side of the field came an opposing shout: "Counter-attack!" From their hiding places a horde of children—Jonas recognized Fiona in the group—emerged, running in a crouched position, firing across the field. Several of them stopped, grabbed their own shoulders and chests with exaggerated gestures, and pretended to be hit. They dropped to the ground and lay suppressing giggles.

Feelings surged within Jonas. He found himself walking forward into the field.

"You're hit, Jonas!" Asher yelled from behind the tree "Pow! You're hit again!"

Jonas stood alone in the center of the field. Several of the children raised their heads and looked at him uneasily. The attacking armies slowed, emerged from their crouched positions, and watched to see what he was doing.

In his mind, Jonas saw again the face of the boy who had lain dying on a field and had begged him for water. He had a sudden choking feeling, as if it were difficult to breathe.

One of the children raised an imaginary rifle and made an attempt to destroy him with a firing noise. "Pssheeew!" Then they were all silent, standing awkwardly, and the only sound was the sound of Jonas's shuddering breaths. He was struggling not to cry.

Gradually, when nothing happened, nothing changed, the children looked at each other nervously and went away. He heard the sounds as they righted their bicycles and began to ride down the path that led from the field.

Only Asher and Fiona remained.

"What's wrong, Jonas? It was only a game," Fiona said.

"You ruined it," Asher said in an irritated voice.

"Don't play it anymore," Jonas pleaded.

"I'm the one who's training for Assistant Recreation Director," Asher pointed out angrily. "Games aren't *your* area of expertness."

"Expertise," Jonas corrected him automatically.

"Whatever. You can't say what we play, even if you *are* going to be the new Receiver." Asher looked warily at him. "I apologize for not paying you the respect you deserve," he mumbled.

"Asher," Jonas said. He was trying to speak carefully, and with kindness, to say exactly what he wanted to say. "You had no way of knowing this. I didn't know it myself until recently. But it's a cruel game. In the past, there have—"

"I said I *apologize*, Jonas."

Jonas sighed. It was no use. Of course Asher couldn't understand. "I accept your apology, Asher," he said wearily.

"Do you want to go for a ride along the river, Jonas?" Fiona asked, biting her lip with nervousness.

Jonas looked at her. She was so lovely. For a fleeting instant he thought he would like nothing better than to ride peacefully along the river path, laughing and talking with his gentle female friend. But he knew that such times had been taken from him now. He shook his head. After a moment his two friends turned and went to their bikes. He watched as they rode away.

Jonas trudged to the bench beside the Storehouse and sat down, overwhelmed with feelings of loss. His childhood, his friendships, his carefree sense of security—all of these things seemed to be slipping away. With his new, heightened feelings, he was overwhelmed by sadness at the way the others had laughed and shouted, playing at war. But he knew that they could not understand why, without the memories. He felt such love for Asher and for Fiona. But they could not feel it back, without the memories. And he could not give them those. Jonas knew with certainty that he could change nothing.

Back in their dwelling, that evening, Lily chattered merrily about the wonderful holiday she had had, playing with her friends, having her midday meal out of doors and (she confessed) sneaking a very short try on her father's bicycle.

"I can't wait til I get my very own bicycle next month. Father's is too big for me. I fell," she explained matter-of-factly. "Good thing Gabe wasn't in the child seat!"

"A very good thing," Mother agreed, frowning at the idea of it. Gabriel waved his arms at the mention of himself. He had begun to walk just the week before. The first steps of a newchild were always the occasion for celebration at the Nurturing Center, Father said, but also for the introduction of a discipline wand. Now Father brought the slender instrument home with him each night, in case Gabriel misbehaved.

But he was a happy and easygoing toddler. Now he moved unsteadily across the room, laughing. "Gay!" he chirped. "Gay!" It was the way he said his own name.

Jonas brightened. It had been a depressing day for him, after such a bright start. But he set his glum thoughts aside. He thought about starting to teach Lily to ride so that she could speed off proudly after her Ceremony of Nine, which would be coming soon. It was hard to believe that it was almost December again, that almost a year had passed since he had become a Twelve.

He smiled as he watched the newchild plant one small foot carefully before the other, grinning with glee at his own steps as he tried them out.

"I want to get to sleep early tonight," Father said. "Tomorrow's a busy day for me. The twins are being born tomorrow, and the test results show that they're identical."

"One for here, one for Elsewhere," Lily chanted. "One for here, one for Else—"

"Do you actually *take* it Elsewhere, Father?" Jonas asked.

"No, I just have to make the selection. I weigh them, hand the larger over to a Nurturer who's standing by, waiting, and then I get the smaller one all cleaned up and comfy. Then I perform a small Ceremony of Release and—" He glanced down, grinning at Gabriel. "Then I wave bye-bye," he said, in the special sweet voice he used when he spoke to the newchild. He waved his hand in the familiar gesture.

Gabriel giggled and waved bye-bye back to him.

"And somebody else comes to get him? Somebody from Elsewhere?"

"That's right, Jonas-bonus."

Jonas rolled his eyes in embarrassment that his father had used the silly pet name.

Lily was deep in thought. "What if they give the little twin a name Elsewhere, a name like, oh, maybe

Jonathan? And here, in our community, at his naming, the twin that we kept here is given the name Jonathan, and then there would be two children with the same name, and they would *look* exactly the same, and someday, maybe when they were a Six, one group of Sixes would go to visit another community on a bus, and there in the other community, in the *other* group of Sixes, would be a Jonathan who was exactly the same as the *other* Jonathan, and then maybe they would get mixed up and take the wrong Jonathan home, and maybe his parents wouldn't notice, and then—"

She paused for breath.

"Lily," Mother said, "I have a wonderful idea. Maybe when you become a Twelve, they'll give you the Assignment of Storyteller! I don't think we've had a Storyteller in the community for a long time. But if I were on the committee, I would definitely choose you for that job!"

Lily grinned. "I have a *better* idea for one more story," she announced. "What if actually we were *all* twins and didn't know it, and so Elsewhere there would be another Lily, and another Jonas, and another Father, and another Asher, and another Chief Elder, and another—"

Father groaned. "Lily," he said. "It's bedtime."

Chapter 18

"Giver," Jonas asked the next afternoon, "do you ever think about release?"

"Do you mean my own release, or just the general topic of release?"

"Both, I guess. I apologi—I mean I should have been more precise. But I don't know exactly what I meant."

"Sit back up. No need to lie down while we're talking." Jonas, who had already been stretched out on the bed when the question came to his mind, sat back up.

"I guess I do think about it occasionally," The Giver said. "I think about my own release when I'm in an awful lot of pain. I wish I could put in a request for it, sometimes. But I'm not permitted to do that until the new Receiver is trained."

"Me," Jonas said in a dejected voice. He was not looking forward to the end of the training, when he would become the new Receiver. It was clear to him what a terribly difficult and lonely life it was, despite the honor.

"I can't request release either," Jonas pointed out. "It was in my rules."

The Giver laughed harshly. "I know that. They hammered out those rules after the failure ten years ago."

Jonas had heard again and again now, reference to the previous failure. But he still did not know what had happened ten years before. "Giver," he said, "tell me what happened. Please."

The Giver shrugged. "On the surface, it was quite

simple. A Receiver-to-be was selected, the way you were. The selection went smoothly enough. The Ceremony was held, and the selection was made. The crowd cheered, as they did for you. The new Receiver was puzzled and a little frightened, as you were."

"My parents told me it was a female."

The Giver nodded.

Jonas thought of his favorite female, Fiona, and shivered. He wouldn't want his gentle friend to suffer the way he had, taking on the memories. "What was she like?" he asked The Giver.

The Giver looked sad, thinking about it. "She was a remarkable young woman. Very self-possessed and serene. Intelligent, eager to learn." He shook his head and drew a deep breath. "You know, Jonas, when she came to me in this room, when she presented herself to begin her training—"

Jonas interrupted him with a question. "Can you tell me her name? My parents said that it wasn't to be spoken again in the community. But couldn't you say it just to me?"

The Giver hesitated painfully, as if saying the name aloud might be excruciating. "Her name was Rosemary," he told Jonas, finally.

"Rosemary. I like that name."

The Giver went on. "When she came to me for the first time, she sat there in the chair where you sat on your first day. She was eager and excited and a little scared. We talked. I tried to explain things as well as I could."

"The way you did to me."

The Giver chuckled ruefully. "The explanations are difficult. The whole thing is so beyond one's experience. But I tried. And she listened carefully. Her eyes were very luminous, I remember."

He looked up suddenly. "Jonas, I gave you a memory that I told you was my favorite. I still have a shred of it left. The room, with the family, and grandparents?"

Jonas nodded. Of course he remembered. "Yes," he said. "It had that wonderful feeling with it. You told me it was love."

"You can understand, then, that that's what I felt for Rosemary," The Giver explained. "I loved her.

"I feel it for you, too," he added.

"What happened to her?" Jonas asked.

"Her training began. She received well, as you do. She was so enthusiastic. So delighted to experience new things. I remember her laughter. . . "

His voice faltered and trailed off.

"What happened?" Jonas asked again, after a moment. "Please tell me."

The Giver closed his eyes. "It broke my heart, Jonas, to transfer pain to her. But it was my job. It was what I had to do, the way I've had to do it to you."

The room was silent. Jonas waited. Finally The Giver continued.

"Five weeks. That was all. I gave her happy memories: a ride on a merry-go-round; a kitten to play with; a picnic. Sometimes I chose one just because I knew it would make her laugh, and I so treasured the sound of that laughter in this room that had always been so silent.

"But she was like you, Jonas. She wanted to experience everything. She knew that it was her responsibility. And so she asked me for more difficult memories."

Jonas held his breath for a moment. "You didn't give her *war*, did you? Not after just five weeks?"

The Giver shook his head and sighed. "No. And I

didn't give her physical pain. But I gave her loneliness. And I gave her loss. I transferred a memory of a child taken from its parents. That was the first one. She appeared stunned at its end."

Jonas swallowed. Rosemary, and her laughter, had begun to seem real to him, and he pictured her looking up from the bed of memories, shocked.

The Giver continued. "I backed off, gave her more little delights. But everything changed, once she knew about pain. I could see it in her eyes."

"She wasn't brave enough?" Jonas suggested.

The Giver didn't respond to the question. "She insisted that I continue, that I not spare her. She said it was her duty. And I knew, of course, that she was correct.

"I couldn't bring myself to inflict physical pain on her. But I gave her anguish of many kinds. Poverty, hunger, and terror.

"I *had* to, Jonas. It was my job. And she had been chosen." The Giver looked at him imploringly. Jonas stroked his hand.

"Finally one afternoon, we finished for the day. It had been a hard session. I tried to finish—as I do with you—by transferring something happy and cheerful. But the times of laughter were gone by then. She stood up very silently, frowning, as if she were making a decision. Then she came over to me and put her arms around me. She kissed my cheek." As Jonas watched, The Giver stroked his own cheek, recalling the touch of Rosemary's lips ten years before.

"She left here that day, left this room, and did not go back to her dwelling. I was notified by the Speaker that she had gone directly to the Chief Elder and asked to be released."

"But it's against the rules! The Receiver-in-training can't apply for rel—"

"It's in your rules, Jonas. But it wasn't in hers. She asked for release, and they had to give it to her. I never saw her again."

So that was the failure, Jonas thought. It was obvious that it saddened The Giver very deeply. But it didn't seem such a terrible thing, after all. And he, Jonas, would never have done it—never have requested release, no matter how difficult his training became. The Giver needed a successor, and he had been chosen.

A thought occurred to Jonas. Rosemary had been released very early in her training. What if something happened to him, Jonas? He had a whole year's worth of memories now.

"Giver?" he asked, "I can't request release, I know that. But what if something happened: an accident? What if I fell into the river like the little Four, Caleb, did? Well, that doesn't make sense because I'm a good swimmer. But what if I couldn't swim, and fell into the river and was lost? Then there wouldn't be a new Receiver, but you would already have given away an awful lot of important memories, so even though they would select a new Receiver, the memories would be gone except for the shreds that you have left of them? And then what if—"

He started to laugh, suddenly. "I sound like my sister, Lily," he said, amused at himself.

The Giver looked at him gravely. "You just stay away from the river, my friend," he said. "The community lost Rosemary after five weeks and it was a disaster for them. I don't know *what* the community would do if they lost you."

"Why was it a disaster?"

"I think I mentioned to you once," The Giver reminded him, "that when she was gone, the memories came back to the people. If you were to be lost in the river, Jonas, your memories would not be lost with you. Memories are *forever*.

"Rosemary had only those five weeks worth, and most of them were good ones. But there were those few terrible memories, the ones that had over-whelmed her. For a while they overwhelmed the community. All those *feelings!* They'd never experienced that before.

"I was so devastated by my own grief at her loss, and my own feeling of failure, that I didn't even try to help them through it. I was angry, too."

The Giver was quiet for a moment, obviously thinking. "You know," he said, finally, "if they lost *you,* with all the training you've had now, they'd have all those memories again themselves."

Jonas made a face. "They'd hate that."

"They certainly would. They wouldn't know how to deal with it at all."

"The only way *I* deal with it is by having you there to help me," Jonas pointed out with a sigh.

The Giver nodded. "I suppose," he said slowly, "that I could—"

"You could what?"

The Giver was still deep in thought. After a moment, he said, "If you floated off in the river, I suppose I could help the whole community the way I've helped you. It's an interesting concept. I need to think about it some more. Maybe we'll talk about it again sometime. But not now.

"I'm glad you're a good swimmer, Jonas. But stay away from the river." He laughed a little, but the laughter was not lighthearted. His thoughts seemed to be elsewhere, and his eyes were very troubled.

Chapter 19

Jonas glanced at the clock. There was so much work to be done, always, that he and The Giver seldom simply sat and talked, the way they just had.

"I'm sorry that I wasted so much time with my questions," Jonas said. "I was only asking about release because my father is releasing a newchild today. A twin. He has to select one and release the other one. They do it by weight." Jonas glanced at the clock. "Actually, I suppose he's already finished. I think it was this morning."

The Giver's face took on a solemn look. "I wish they wouldn't do that," he said quietly, almost to himself.

"Well, they can't have two identical people around! Think how confusing it would be!" Jonas chuckled.

"I wish I could watch," he added, as an afterthought. He liked the thought of seeing his father perform the ceremony, and making the little twin clean and comfy. His father was such a gentle man.

"You can watch," The Giver said.

"No," Jonas told him. "They never let children watch. It's very private."

"Jonas," The Giver told him, "I know that you recall your training instructions very carefully. Don't you remember that you are allowed to ask anyone anything?"

Jonas nodded. "Yes, but—"

"Jonas, when you and I have finished our time together, you will be the new Receiver. You can read the books; you'll have the memories. You have access to *everything*. It's part of your training. If you want to watch a release, you have simply to ask."

Jonas shrugged. "Well, maybe I will, then. But it's too late for this one. I'm sure it was this morning."

The Giver told him, then, something he had not known. "All private ceremonies are recorded. They're in the Hall of Closed Records. *Do you want to see this morning's release?*"

Jonas hesitated. He was afraid that his father wouldn't like it, if he watched something so private.

"I think you should," The Giver told him firmly.

"All right, then," Jonas said. "Tell me how."

The Giver rose from his chair, went to the speaker on the wall, and clicked the switch from OFF to ON.

The voice spoke immediately. "Yes, Receiver. How may I help you?"

"I would like to see this morning's release of the twin."

"One moment, Receiver. Thank you for your instructions."

Jonas watched the video screen above the row of switches. Its blank face began to flicker with zig-zag lines; then some numbers appeared, followed by the date and time. He was astonished and delighted that this was available to him, and surprised that he had not known.

Suddenly he could see a small windowless room, empty except for a bed, a table with some equipment on it—Jonas recognized a scale; he had seen them before, when he'd been doing volunteer hours at the Nurturing Center—and a cupboard. He could see pale carpeting on the floor.

"It's just an ordinary room," he commented. "I thought maybe they'd have it in the Auditorium, so that everybody could come. All the Old go to

Ceremonies of Release. But I suppose that when it's just a newborn, they don't—"

"Shhh," The Giver said, his eyes on the screen.

Jonas's father, wearing his nurturing uniform, entered the room, cradling a tiny newchild wrapped in a soft blanket in his arms. A uniformed woman followed through the door, carrying a second newchild wrapped in a similar blanket.

"That's my father." Jonas found himself whispering, as if he might wake the little ones if he spoke aloud. "And the other Nurturer is his assistant. She's still in training, but she'll be finished soon."

These two Nurturers unwrapped the blankets and laid the identical newborns on the bed. They were naked. Jonas could see that they were males.

He watched, fascinated, as his father gently lifted one and then the other to the scale and weighed them.

He heard his father laugh. "Good," his father said to the woman. "I thought for a moment that they might both be exactly the same. *Then* we'd have a problem. But this one," he handed one, after rewrapping it, to his assistant, "is six pounds even. So you can clean him up and dress him and take him over to the Center."

The woman took the newchild and left through the door she had entered.

Jonas watched as his father bent over the squirming newchild on the bed. "And you, little guy, you're only five pounds ten ounces. A *shrimp!*"

"That's the special voice he uses with Gabriel," Jonas remarked, smiling.

"Watch," The Giver said.

"Now he cleans him up and makes him comfy," Jonas told him. "He told me."

"Be quiet, Jonas," The Giver commanded in a strange voice. "*Watch.*"

Obediently Jonas concentrated on the screen, waiting for what would happen next. He was especially curious about the ceremony part.

His father turned and opened the cupboard. He took out a syringe and a small bottle. Very carefully he inserted the needle into the bottle and began to fill the syringe with a clear liquid.

Jonas winced sympathetically. He had forgotten that newchildren had to get shots. He hated shots himself, though he knew that they were necessary.

To his surprise, his father began very carefully to direct the needle into the top of the newchild's forehead, puncturing the place where the fragile skin pulsed. The newborn squirmed, and wailed faintly.

"Why's he—"

"Shhh," The Giver said sharply.

His father was talking, and Jonas realized that he was hearing the answer to the question he had started to ask. Still in the special voice, his father was saying, "I know, I know. It hurts, little guy. But I have to use a vein, and the veins in your arms are still too teeny-weeny."

He pushed the plunger very slowly, injecting the liquid into the scalp vein until the syringe was empty.

"All done. That wasn't so bad, was it?" Jonas heard his father say cheerfully. He turned aside and dropped the syringe into a waste receptacle.

Now he cleans him up and makes him comfy, Jonas said to himself, aware that The Giver didn't want to talk during the little ceremony.

As he continued to watch, the newchild, no longer crying, moved his arms and legs in a jerking motion. Then he went limp. His head fell to the side, his eyes half open. Then he was still.

With an odd, shocked feeling, Jonas recognized the gestures and posture and expression. They were familiar. He had seen them before. But he couldn't remember where.

Jonas stared at the screen, waiting for something to happen. But nothing did. The little twin lay motionless. His father was putting things away. Folding the blanket. Closing the cupboard.

Once again, as he had on the playing field, he felt the choking sensation. Once again he saw the face of the light-haired, bloodied soldier as life left his eyes. The memory came back.

He killed it! My father killed it! Jonas said to himself, stunned at what he was realizing. He continued to stare at the screen numbly.

His father tidied the room. Then he picked up a small carton that lay waiting on the floor, set it on the bed, and lifted the limp body into it. He placed the lid on tightly.

He picked up the carton and carried it to the other side of the room. He opened a small door in the wall; Jonas could see darkness behind the door. It seemed to be the same sort of chute into which trash was deposited at school.

His father loaded the carton containing the body into the chute and gave it a shove.

"Bye-bye, little guy," Jonas heard his father say before he left the room. Then the screen went blank.

The Giver turned to him. Quite calmly, he related, "When the Speaker notified me that Rosemary had applied for release, they turned on the tape to show me the process. There she was—my last glimpse of that beautiful child—waiting. They brought in the syringe and asked her to roll up her sleeve.

"You suggested, Jonas, that perhaps she wasn't brave enough? I don't know about bravery: what it is, what it means. I do know that I sat here numb with horror. Wretched with helplessness. And I listened as Rosemary told them that she would prefer to inject herself.

"Then she did so. I didn't watch. I looked away."

The Giver turned to him. "Well, there you are, Jonas. You were wondering about release," he said in a bitter voice.

Jonas felt a ripping sensation inside himself, the feeling of terrible pain clawing its way forward to emerge in a cry.

Chapter 20

"I won't! I won't go home! You can't make me!" Jonas sobbed and shouted and pounded the bed with his fists.

"Sit up, Jonas," The Giver told him firmly.

Jonas obeyed him. Weeping, shuddering, he sat on the edge of the bed. He would not look at The Giver.

"You may stay here tonight. I want to talk to you. But you must be quiet now, while I notify your family unit. No one must hear you cry."

Jonas looked up wildly. "No one heard that little twin cry, either. No one but my father!" He collapsed in sobs again.

The Giver waited silently. Finally Jonas was able to quiet himself, and he sat huddled, his shoulders shaking.

The Giver went to the wall speaker and clicked the switch to ON.

"Yes, Receiver. How may I help you?"

"Notify the new Receiver's family unit that he will be staying with me tonight, for additional training."

"I will take care of that, sir. Thank you for your instructions," the voice said.

"I will take care of that, sir. I will take care of that, sir," Jonas mimicked in a cruel, sarcastic voice. "I will do whatever you like, sir. I will kill people, sir. Old people? Small newborn people? I'd be happy to kill them, sir. Thank you for your instructions, sir. How may I help y—" He couldn't seem to stop.

The Giver grasped his shoulders firmly. Jonas fell silent and stared at him.

"Listen to me, Jonas. They can't help it. *They know nothing.*"

"You said that to me once before."

"I said it because it's true. It's the way they live. It's the life that was created for them. It's the same life that you would have, if you had not been chosen as my successor."

"But he *lied* to me!" Jonas wept.

"It's what he was told to do, and he knows nothing else."

"What about you? Do you lie to me, too?" Jonas almost spat the question at The Giver.

"I am empowered to lie. But I have never lied to you."

Jonas stared at him. "Release is always like that? For people who break the rules three times? For the *Old*? Do they kill the Old, too?"

"Yes, it's true."

"And what about Fiona? She loves the Old! She's in training to care for them. Does she know yet? What will she do when she finds out? How will she feel?" Jonas brushed wetness from his face with the back of one hand.

"Fiona is already being trained in the fine art of release," The Giver told him. "She's very efficient at her work, your red-haired friend. Feelings are not part of the life she's learned."

Jonas wrapped his arms around himself and rocked his own body back and forth. "What should I do? I can't go back! I can't!"

The Giver stood up. "First, I will order our evening meal. Then we will eat."

Jonas found himself using the nasty, sarcastic voice again. "Then we'll have a sharing of feelings?"

The Giver gave a rueful, anguished, empty laugh. "Jonas, you and I are the only ones who *have* feelings. We've been sharing them now for almost a year."

"I'm sorry, Giver," Jonas said miserably. "I don't mean to be so hateful. Not to you."

The Giver rubbed Jonas's hunched shoulders. "And after we eat," he went on, "we'll make a plan."

Jonas looked up, puzzled. "A plan for what? There's nothing. There's nothing we can do. It's always been this way. Before me, before you, before the ones who came before you. Back and back and back." His voice trailed the familiar phrase.

"Jonas," The Giver said, after a moment, "it's true that it has been this way for what seems forever. But the memories tell us that it has not *always* been. People felt things once. You and I have been part of that, so we know. We know that they once had felt things like pride, and sorrow, and—"

"And love," Jonas added, remembering the family scene that had so affected him. "And pain." He thought again of the soldier.

"The worst part of holding the memories is not the pain. It's the loneliness of it. Memories need to be shared."

"I've started to share them with you," Jonas said, trying to cheer him.

"That's true. And having you here with me over the past year has made me realize that things must change. For years I've felt that they should, but it seemed so hopeless.

"Now for the first time I think there might be a way," The Giver said slowly. "And you brought it to my attention, barely—" He glanced at the clock, "two hours ago."

Jonas watched him, and listened.

It was late at night, now. They had talked and

talked. Jonas sat wrapped in a robe belonging to The Giver, the long robe that only Elders wore.

It was possible, what they had planned. Barely possible. If it failed, he would very likely be killed.

But what did that matter? If he stayed, his life was no longer worth living.

"Yes," he told The Giver. "I'll do it. I think I can do it. I'll try, anyway. But I want you to come with me."

The Giver shook his head. "Jonas," he said, "the community has depended, all these generations, back and back and back, on a resident Receiver to hold their memories for them. I've turned over many of them to you in the past year. And I can't take them back. There's no way for me to get them back if I have given them.

"So if you escape, once you are gone—and, Jonas, you know that you can never return—"

Jonas nodded solemnly. It was the terrifying part. "Yes," he said, "I know. But if you come with me—"

The Giver shook his head and made a gesture to silence him. He continued. "If you get away, if you get beyond, if you get to Elsewhere, it will mean that the community has to bear the burden themselves, of the memories you had been holding for them.

"I think that they can, and that they will acquire some wisdom. But it will be desperately hard for them. When we lost Rosemary ten years ago, and her memories returned to the people, they panicked. And those were such few memories, compared to yours. When your memories return, they'll need help. Remember how I helped you in the beginning, when the receiving of memories was new to you?"

Jonas nodded. "It was scary at first. And it hurt a lot."

"You needed me then. And now they will."

"It's no use. They'll find someone to take my place. They'll choose a new Receiver."

"There's no one ready for training, not right away. Oh, they'll speed up the selection, of course. But I can't think of another child who has the right qualities—"

"There's a little female with pale eyes. But she's only a Six."

"That's correct. I know the one you mean. Her name is Katharine. But she's too young. So they will be *forced* to bear those memories."

"I want you to come, Giver," Jonas pleaded.

"No. I have to stay here," The Giver said firmly. "I want to, Jonas. If I go with you, and together we take away *all* their protection from the memories, Jonas, the community will be left with no one to help them. They'll be thrown into chaos. They'll destroy themselves. I can't go."

"Giver," Jonas suggested, "you and I don't need to *care* about the rest of them."

The Giver looked at him with a questioning smile. Jonas hung his head. Of course they needed to care. It was the meaning of everything.

"And in any case, Jonas," The Giver sighed, "I wouldn't make it. I'm very weakened now. Do you know that I no longer see colors?"

Jonas's heart broke. He reached for The Giver's hand.

"You have the colors," The Giver told him. "And you have the courage. I will help you to have the strength."

"A year ago," Jonas reminded him, "when I had just become a Twelve, when I began to see the first color, you told me that the beginning had been different for you. But that I wouldn't understand."

The Giver brightened. "That's true. And do you

know, Jonas, that with all your knowledge now, with all your memories, with all you've learned—*still* you won't understand? Because I've been a little selfish. I haven't given any of it to you. I wanted to keep it for myself to the last."

"Keep what?"

"When I was just a boy, younger than you, it began to come to me. But it wasn't the seeing-beyond for me. It was different. For me, it was *hearing*-beyond."

Jonas frowned, trying to figure that out. "What did you hear?" he asked.

"Music," The Giver said, smiling. "I began to hear something truly remarkable, and it is called music. I'll give you some before I go."

Jonas shook his head emphatically. "No, Giver," he said. "I want you to keep that, to have with you, when I'm gone."

Jonas went home the next morning, cheerfully greeted his parents, and lied easily about what a busy, pleasant night he had had.

His father smiled and lied easily, too, about his busy and pleasant day the day before.

Throughout the school day, as he did his lessons, Jonas went over the plan in his head. It seemed startlingly simple. Jonas and The Giver had gone over it and over it, late into the night hours.

For the next two weeks, as the time for the December Ceremony approached, The Giver would transfer every memory of courage and strength that he could to Jonas. He would need those to help him find the Elsewhere that they were both sure existed. They knew it would be a very difficult journey.

Then, in the middle of the night before the Ceremony, Jonas would secretly leave his dwelling.

This was probably the most dangerous part, because it was a violation of a major rule for any citizen not on official business to leave a dwelling at night.

"I'll leave at midnight," Jonas said. "The Food Collectors will be finished picking up the evening-meal remains by then, and the Path-Maintenance Crews don't start their work that early. So there won't be anyone to see me, unless of course someone is out on emergency business."

"I don't know what you should do if you are seen, Jonas," The Giver had said. "I have memories, of course, of all kinds of escapes. People fleeing from terrible things throughout history. But every situation is individual. There is no memory of one like this."

"I'll be careful," Jonas said. "No one will see me."

"As Receiver-in-training, you're held in very high respect already. So I think you wouldn't be questioned very forcefully."

"I'd just say I was on some important errand for the Receiver. I'd say it was all your fault that I was out after hours," Jonas teased.

They both laughed a little nervously. But Jonas was certain that he could slip away, unseen, from his house, carrying an extra set of clothing. Silently he would take his bicycle to the riverbank and leave it there hidden in bushes with the clothing folded beside it.

Then he would make his way through the darkness, on foot, silently, to the Annex.

"There's no nighttime attendant," The Giver explained. "I'll leave the door unlocked. You simply slip into the room. I'll be waiting for you."

His parents would discover, when they woke, that he was gone. They would also find a cheerful note from Jonas on his bed, telling them that he was going for an early morning ride along the river; that he would be back for the Ceremony.

His parents would be irritated but not alarmed. They would think him inconsiderate and they would plan to chastise him, later.

They would wait, with mounting anger, for him; finally they would be forced to go, taking Lily to the Ceremony without him.

"They won't say anything to anyone, though," Jonas said, quite certain. "They won't call attention to my rudeness because it would reflect on their parenting. And anyway, everyone is so involved in the Ceremony that they probably won't notice that I'm not there. Now that I'm a Twelve and in training, I don't have to sit with my age group any more. So Asher will think I'm with my parents, or with you—"

"And your parents will assume you're with Asher, or with me—"

Jonas shrugged. "It will take everyone a while to realize that I'm not there at all."

"And you and I will be long on our way by then."

In the early morning, The Giver would order a vehicle and driver from the Speaker. He visited the other communities frequently, meeting with their Elders; his responsibilities extended over all the surrounding areas. So this would not be an unusual undertaking.

Ordinarily The Giver did not attend the December Ceremony. Last year he had been present because of the occasion of Jonas's selection, in which he was so involved. But his life was usually quite separate from that of the community. No one would comment on his absence, or on the fact that he had chosen this day to be away.

When the driver and vehicle arrived, The Giver would send the driver on some brief errand. During his absence, The Giver would help Jonas hide in the storage area of the vehicle. He would have with him a bundle of food which The Giver would save from his own meals during the next two weeks.

The Ceremony would begin, with all the community there, and by then Jonas and The Giver would be on their way.

By midday Jonas's absence would become apparent, and would be a cause for serious concern. The Ceremony would not be disrupted—such a disruption would be unthinkable. But searchers would be sent out into the community.

By the time his bicycle and clothing were found, The Giver would be returning. Jonas, by then, would be on his own, making his journey Elsewhere.

The Giver, on his return, would find the community in a state of confusion and panic. Confronted by a situation which they had never faced before, and having no memories from which to find either solace or wisdom, they would not know what to do and would seek his advice.

He would go to the Auditorium where the people would be gathered, still. He would stride to the stage and command their attention.

He would make the solemn announcement that Jonas had been lost in the river. He would immediately begin the Ceremony of Loss.

"Jonas, Jonas," they would say loudly, as they had once said the name of Caleb. The Giver would lead the chant. Together they would let Jonas's presence in their lives fade away as they said his name in unison more slowly, softer and softer, until he was disappearing from them, until he was no more than an occasional murmur and then, by the end of the long day, gone forever, not to be mentioned again.

Their attention would turn to the overwhelming

task of bearing the memories themselves. The Giver would help them.

"Yes, I understand that they'll need you," Jonas had said at the end of the lengthy discussion and planning. "But I'll need you, too. Please come with me." He knew the answer even as he made the final plea.

"My work will be finished," The Giver had replied gently, "when I have helped the community to change and become whole.

"I'm grateful to you, Jonas, because without you I would never have figured out a way to bring about the change. But your role now is to escape. And my role is to stay."

"But don't you *want* to be with me, Giver?" Jonas asked sadly.

The Giver hugged him. "I love you, Jonas," he said. "But I have another place to go. When my work here is finished, I want to be with my daughter."

Jonas had been staring glumly at the floor. Now he looked up, startled. "I didn't know you had a daughter, Giver. You told me that you'd had a spouse. But I never knew about your daughter."

The Giver smiled, and nodded. For the first time in their long months together, Jonas saw him look truly happy.

"Her name was Rosemary," The Giver said.

Chapter 21

It would work. They could make it work, Jonas told himself again and again throughout the day.

But that evening everything changed. All of it—all the things they had thought through so meticulously—fell apart.

That night, Jonas was forced to flee. He left the dwelling shortly after the sky became dark and the community still. It was terribly dangerous because some of the work crews were still about, but he moved stealthily and silently, staying in the shadows, making his way past the darkened dwellings and the empty Central Plaza, toward the river. Beyond the Plaza he could see the House of the Old, with the Annex behind it, outlined against the night sky. But he could not stop there. There was no time. Every minute counted now, and every minute must take him farther from the community.

Now he was on the bridge, hunched over on the bicycle, pedaling steadily. He could see the dark, churning water far below.

He felt, surprisingly, no fear, nor any regret at leaving the community behind. But he felt a very deep sadness that he had left his closest friend behind. He knew that in the danger of his escape he must be absolutely silent; but with his heart and mind, he called back and hoped that with his capacity for hearing-beyond, The Giver would know that Jonas had said goodbye.

It had happened at the evening meal. The family

unit was eating together as always: Lily chattering away, Mother and Father making their customary comments (and lies, Jonas knew) about the day. Nearby, Gabriel played happily on the floor, babbling his baby talk, looking with glee now and then toward Jonas, obviously delighted to have him back after the unexpected night away from the dwelling.

Father glanced down toward the toddler. "Enjoy it, little guy," he said. "This is your last night as a visitor."

"What do you mean?" Jonas asked him.

Father sighed with disappointment. "Well, you know he wasn't here when you got home this morning because we had him stay overnight at the Nurturing Center. It seemed like a good opportunity, with you gone, to give it a try. He'd been sleeping so soundly."

"Didn't it go well?" Mother asked sympathetically.

Father gave a rueful laugh. "That's an understatement. It was a disaster. He cried all night, apparently. The night crew couldn't handle it. They were *really* frazzled by the time I got to work."

"Gabe, you naughty thing," Lily said, with a scolding little cluck toward the grinning toddler on the floor.

"So," Father went on, "we obviously had to make the decision. Even *I* voted for Gabriel's release when we had the meeting this afternoon."

Jonas put down his fork and stared at his father. "Release?" he asked.

Father nodded. "We certainly gave it our best try, didn't we?"

"Yes, we did," Mother agreed emphatically.

Lily nodded in agreement, too.

Jonas worked at keeping his voice absolutely calm. "When?" he asked. "When will he be released?"

"First thing tomorrow morning. We have to start our preparations for the Naming Ceremony, so we thought we'd get this taken care of right away.

"It's bye-bye to you, Gabe, in the morning," Father had said, in his sweet, sing-song voice.

Jonas reached the opposite side of the river, stopped briefly, and looked back. The community where his entire life had been lived lay behind him now, sleeping. At dawn, the orderly, disciplined life he had always known would continue again, without him. The life where nothing was ever unexpected. Or inconvenient. Or unusual. The life without color, pain, or past.

He pushed firmly again at the pedal with his foot and continued riding along the road. It was not safe to spend time looking back. He thought of the rules he had broken so far: enough that if he were caught, now, he would be condemned.

First, he had left the dwelling at night. A major transgression.

Second, he had robbed the community of food: a very serious crime, even though what he had taken was leftovers, set out on the dwelling doorsteps for collection.

Third, he had stolen his father's bicycle. He had hesitated for a moment, standing beside the bikeport in the darkness, not wanting anything of his father's and uncertain, as well, whether he could comfortably ride the larger bike when he was so accustomed to his own.

But it was necessary because it had the child seat attached to the back.

And he had taken Gabriel, too.

He could feel the little head nudge his back, bouncing gently against him as he rode. Gabriel was sleeping soundly, strapped into the seat. Before he had left the dwelling, he had laid his hands firmly on Gabe's back and transmitted to him the most soothing memory he could: a slow-swinging hammock under palm trees on an island someplace, at evening, with a rhythmic sound of languid water lapping hypnotically against a beach nearby. As the memory seeped from him into the newchild, he could feel Gabe's sleep ease and deepen. There had been no stir at all when Jonas lifted him from the crib and placed him gently into the molded seat.

He knew that he had the remaining hours of night before they would be aware of his escape. So he rode hard, steadily, willing himself not to tire as the minutes and miles passed. There had been no time to receive the memories he and The Giver had counted on, of strength and courage. So he relied on what he had, and hoped it would be enough.

He circled the outlying communities, their dwellings dark. Gradually the distances between communities widened, with longer stretches of empty road. His legs ached at first; then, as time passed, they became numb.

At dawn Gabriel began to stir. They were in an isolated place; fields on either side of the road were dotted with thickets of trees here and there. He saw a stream, and made his way to it across a rutted, bumpy meadow; Gabriel, wide awake now, giggled as the bicycle jolted him up and down.

Jonas unstrapped Gabe, lifted him from the bike, and watched him investigate the grass and twigs with delight. Carefully he hid the bicycle in thick bushes.

"Morning meal, Gabe!" He unwrapped some of the food and fed them both. Then he filled the cup he had brought with water from the stream and held it for Gabriel to drink. He drank thirstily himself, and sat by the stream, watching the newchild play.

He was exhausted. He knew he must sleep, resting his own muscles and preparing himself for more hours on the bicycle. It would not be safe to travel in daylight.

They would be looking for him soon.

He found a place deeply hidden in the trees, took the newchild there, and lay down, holding Gabriel in his arms. Gabe struggled cheerfully as if it were a wrestling game, the kind they had played back in the dwelling, with tickles and laughter.

"Sorry, Gabe," Jonas told him. "I know it's morning, and I know you just woke up. But we have to sleep now."

He cuddled the small body close to him, and rubbed the little back. He murmured to Gabriel soothingly. Then he pressed his hands firmly and transmitted a memory of deep, contented exhaustion. Gabriel's head nodded, after a moment, and fell against Jonas's chest.

Together the fugitives slept through the first dangerous day.

The most terrifying thing was the planes. By now, days had passed; Jonas no longer knew how many. The journey had become automatic: the sleep by days, hidden in underbrush and trees; the finding of water; the careful division of scraps of food, augmented by what he could find in the fields. And the endless, endless miles on the bicycle by night.

His leg muscles were taut now. They ached when he settled himself to sleep. But they were stronger, and he stopped now less often to rest. Sometimes he paused and lifted Gabriel down for a brief bit of exercise, running down the road or through a field together in the dark. But always, when he returned, strapped the uncomplaining toddler into the seat again, and remounted, his legs were ready.

So he had enough strength of his own, and had not needed what The Giver might have provided, had there been time.

But when the planes came, he wished that he could have received the courage.

He knew they were search planes. They flew so low that they woke him with the noise of their engines, and sometimes, looking out and up fearfully from the hiding places, he could almost see the faces of the searchers.

He knew that they could not see color, and that their flesh, as well as Gabriel's light golden curls, would be no more than smears of gray against the colorless foliage. But he remembered from his science and technology studies at school that the search planes used heat-seeking devices which could identify body warmth and would hone in on two humans huddled in shrubbery.

So always, when he heard the aircraft sound, he reached to Gabriel and transmitted memories of snow, keeping some for himself. Together they became cold; and when the planes were gone, they would shiver, holding each other, until sleep came again.

Sometimes, urging the memories into Gabriel, Jonas felt that they were more shallow, a little weaker than they had been. It was what he had hoped, and what he and The Giver had planned: that as he moved away from the community, he would shed the memories and leave them behind for the people. But now, when he needed them, when the planes came, he tried hard to cling to what he still had, of cold, and to use it for their survival.

Usually the aircraft came by day, when they were hiding. But he was alert at night, too, on the road, always listening intently for the sound of the engines. Even Gabriel listened, and would call out, "Plane! Plane!" sometimes before Jonas had heard the terrifying noise. When the aircraft searchers came, as they did occasionally, during the night as they rode, Jonas sped to the nearest tree or bush, dropped to the ground, and made himself and Gabriel cold. But it was sometimes a frighteningly close call.

As he pedaled through the nights, through isolated landscape now, with the communities far behind and no sign of human habitation around him or ahead, he was constantly vigilant, looking for the next nearest hiding place should the sound of engines come.

But the frequency of the planes diminished. They came less often, and flew, when they did come, less slowly, as if the search had become haphazard and no longer hopeful. Finally there was an entire day and night when they did not come at all.

Chapter 22

Now the landscape was changing. It was a subtle change, hard to identify at first. The road was narrower, and bumpy, apparently no longer tended by road crews. It was harder, suddenly, to balance on the bike, as the front wheel wobbled over stones and rocks.

One night Jonas fell, when the bike jolted to a sudden stop against a rock. He grabbed instinctively for Gabriel; and the newchild, strapped tightly in his seat, was uninjured, only frightened when the bike fell to its side. But Jonas's ankle was twisted, and his knees were scraped and raw, blood seeping through his torn trousers. Painfully he righted himself and the bike, and reassured Gabe.

Tentatively he began to ride in daylight. He had forgotten the fear of the searchers, who seemed to have diminished into the past. But now there were new fears; the unfamiliar landscape held hidden, unknown perils.

Trees became more numerous, and the forests beside the road were dark and thick with mystery. They saw streams more frequently now and stopped often to drink. Jonas carefully washed his injured knees, wincing as he rubbed at the raw flesh. The constant ache of his swollen ankle was eased when he soaked it occasionally in the cold water that rushed through roadside gullies.

He was newly aware that Gabriel's safety depended entirely upon his own continued strength.

They saw their first waterfall, and for the first time wildlife.

"Plane! Plane!" Gabriel called, and Jonas turned swiftly into the trees, though he had not seen planes in days, and he did not hear an aircraft engine now. When he stopped the bicycle in the shrubbery and turned to grab Gabe, he saw the small chubby arm pointing toward the sky.

Terrified, he looked up, but it was not a plane at all. Though he had never seen one before, he identified it from his fading memories, for The Giver had given them to him often. It was a bird.

Soon there were many birds along the way, soaring overhead, calling. They saw deer; and once, beside the road, looking at them curious and unafraid, a small reddish-brown creature with a thick tail, whose name Jonas did not know. He slowed the bike and they stared at one another until the creature turned away and disappeared into the woods.

All of it was new to him. After a life of Sameness and predictability, he was awed by the surprises that lay beyond each curve of the road. He slowed the bike again and again to look with wonder at wildflowers, to enjoy the throaty warble of a new bird nearby, or merely to watch the way wind shifted the leaves in the trees. During his twelve years in the community, he had never felt such simple moments of exquisite happiness.

But there were desperate fears building in him now as well. The most relentless of his new fears was that they would starve. Now that they had left the cultivated fields behind them, it was almost impossible to find food. They finished the meager store of potatoes and carrots they had saved from the last agricultural area, and now they were always hungry.

Jonas knelt by a stream and tried without success to catch a fish with his hands. Frustrated, he threw rocks into the water, knowing even as he did so that it was useless. Finally, in desperation, he fashioned a makeshift net, looping the strands of Gabriel's blanket around a curved stick.

After countless tries, the net yielded two flopping silvery fish. Methodically Jonas hacked them to pieces with a sharp rock and fed the raw shreds to himself and to Gabriel. They ate some berries, and tried without success to catch a bird.

At night, while Gabriel slept beside him, Jonas lay awake, tortured by hunger, and remembered his life in the community where meals were delivered to each dwelling every day.

He tried to use the flagging power of his memory to recreate meals, and managed brief, tantalizing fragments: banquets with huge roasted meats; birthday parties with thick-frosted cakes; and lush fruits picked and eaten, sun-warmed and dripping, from trees.

But when the memory glimpses subsided, he was left with the gnawing, painful emptiness. Jonas remembered, suddenly and grimly, the time in his childhood when he had been chastised for misusing a word. The word had been "starving." You have never been starving, he had been told. You will never be starving.

Now he was. If he had stayed in the community, he would not be. It was as simple as that. Once he had yearned for choice. Then, when he had had a choice, he had made the wrong one: the choice to leave. And now he was starving.

But if he had stayed . . .

His thoughts continued. If he had stayed, he would have starved in other ways. He would have lived a life hungry for feelings, for color, for love.

And Gabriel? For Gabriel there would have been

no life at all. So there had not really been a choice.

It became a struggle to ride the bicycle as Jonas weakened from lack of food, and realized at the same time that he was encountering something he had for a long time yearned to see: hills. His sprained ankle throbbed as he forced the pedal downward in an effort that was almost beyond him.

And the weather was changing. It rained for two days. Jonas had never seen rain, though he had experienced it often in the memories. He had liked those rains, enjoyed the new feeling of it, but this was different. He and Gabriel became cold and wet, and it was hard to get dry, even when sunshine occasionally followed.

Gabriel had not cried during the long frightening journey. Now he did. He cried because he was hungry and cold and terribly weak. Jonas cried, too, for the same reasons, and another reason as well. He wept because he was afraid now that he could not save Gabriel. He no longer cared about himself.

Chapter 23

Jonas felt more and more certain that the destination lay ahead of him, very near now in the night that was approaching. None of his senses confirmed it. He saw nothing ahead except the endless ribbon of road unfolding in twisting narrow curves. He heard no sound ahead.

Yet he felt it: felt that Elsewhere was not far away. But he had little hope left that he would be able to reach it. His hope diminished further when the sharp, cold air began to blur and thicken with swirling white.

Gabriel, wrapped in his inadequate blanket, was hunched, shivering, and silent in his little seat. Jonas stopped the bike wearily, lifted the child down, and realized with heartbreak how cold and weak Gabe had become.

Standing in the freezing mound that was thickening around his numb feet, Jonas opened his own tunic, held Gabriel to his bare chest, and tied the torn and dirty blanket around them both. Gabriel moved feebly against him and whimpered briefly into the silence that surrounded them.

Dimly, from a nearly forgotten perception as blurred as the substance itself, Jonas recalled what the whiteness was.

"It's called snow, Gabe," Jonas whispered. "*Snowflakes*. They fall down from the sky, and they're very beautiful."

There was no response from the child who had once been so curious and alert. Jonas looked down through the dusk at the little head against his chest.

Gabriel's curly hair was matted and filthy, and there were tearstains outlined in dirt on his pale cheeks. His eyes were closed. As Jonas watched, a snowflake drifted down and was caught briefly for a moment's sparkle in the tiny fluttering eyelashes.

Wearily he remounted the bicycle. A steep hill loomed ahead. In the best of conditions, the hill would have been a difficult, demanding ride. But now the rapidly deepening snow obscured the narrow road and made the ride impossible. His front wheel moved forward imperceptibly as he pushed on the pedals with his numb, exhausted legs. But the bicycle stopped. It would not move.

He got off and let it drop sideways into the snow. For a moment he thought how easy it would be to drop beside it himself, to let himself and Gabriel slide into the softness of snow, the darkness of night, the warm comfort of sleep.

But he had come this far. He must try to go on.

The memories had fallen behind him now, escaping from his protection to return to the people of his community. Were there any left at all? Could he hold onto a last bit of warmth? Did he still have the strength to Give? Could Gabriel still Receive?

He pressed his hands into Gabriel's back and tried to remember sunshine. For a moment it seemed that nothing came to him, that his power was completely gone. Then it flickered suddenly, and he felt tiny tongues of heat begin to creep across and into his frozen feet and legs. He felt his face begin to glow and the tense, cold skin of his arms and hands relax. For a fleeting second he felt that he wanted to keep it for himself, to let himself bathe in sunlight, unburdened by anything or anyone else.

But the moment passed and was followed by an urge, a need, a passionate yearning to share the warmth with the one person left for him to love. Aching from the effort, he forced the memory of warmth into the thin, shivering body in his arms.

Gabriel stirred. For a moment they both were bathed in warmth and renewed strength as they stood hugging each other in the blinding snow.

Jonas began to walk up the hill.

The memory was agonizingly brief. He had trudged no more than a few yards through the night when it was gone and they were cold again.

But his mind was alert now. Warming himself ever so briefly had shaken away the lethargy and resignation and restored his will to survive. He began to walk faster on feet that he could no longer feel. But the hill was treacherously steep; he was impeded by the snow and his own lack of strength. He didn't make it very far before he stumbled and fell forward.

On his knees, unable to rise, Jonas tried a second time. His consciousness grasped at a wisp of another warm memory, and tried desperately to hold it there, to enlarge it, and pass it into Gabriel. His spirits and strength lifted with the momentary warmth and he stood. Again, Gabriel stirred against him as he began to climb.

But the memory faded, leaving him colder than before.

If only he had had time to receive more warmth from The Giver before he escaped! Maybe there would be more left for him now. But there was no purpose in if-onlys. His entire concentration now had to be on moving his feet, warming Gabriel and himself, and going forward.

He climbed, stopped, and warmed them both briefly again, with a tiny scrap of memory that seemed certainly to be all he had left.

The top of the hill seemed so far away, and he did

not know what lay beyond. But there was nothing left to do but continue. He trudged upward.

As he approached the summit of the hill at last, something began to happen. He was not warmer; if anything, he felt more numb and more cold. He was not less exhausted; on the contrary, his steps were leaden, and he could barely move his freezing, tired legs.

But he began, suddenly, to feel happy. He began to recall happy times. He remembered his parents and his sister. He remembered his friends, Asher and Fiona. He remembered The Giver.

Memories of joy flooded through him suddenly.

He reached the place where the hill crested and he could feel the ground under his snow-covered feet become level. It would not be uphill anymore.

"We're almost there, Gabriel," he whispered, feeling quite certain without knowing why. "I remember this place, Gabe." And it was true. But it was not a grasping of a thin and burdensome recollection; this was different. This was something that he could keep. It was a memory of his own.

He hugged Gabriel and rubbed him briskly, warming him, to keep him alive. The wind was bitterly cold. The snow swirled, blurring his vision. But somewhere ahead, through the blinding storm, he knew there was warmth and light.

Using his final strength, and a special knowledge that was deep inside him, Jonas found the sled that was waiting for them at the top of the hill. Numbly his hands fumbled for the rope.

He settled himself on the sled and hugged Gabe close. The hill was steep but the snow was powdery and soft, and he knew that this time there would be no ice, no fall, no pain. Inside his freezing body, his heart surged with hope.

They started down.

Jonas felt himself losing consciousness and with his whole being willed himself to stay upright atop the sled, clutching Gabriel, keeping him safe. The runners sliced through the snow and the wind whipped at his face as they sped in a straight line through an incision that seemed to lead to the final destination, the place that he had always felt was waiting, the Elsewhere that held their future and their past.

He forced his eyes open as they went downward, downward, sliding, and all at once he could see lights, and he recognized them now. He knew they were shining through the windows of rooms, that they were the red, blue, and yellow lights that twinkled from trees in places where families created and kept memories, where they celebrated love.

Downward, downward, faster and faster. Suddenly he was aware with certainty and joy that below, ahead, they were waiting for him; and that they were waiting, too, for the baby. For the first time, he heard something that he knew to be music. He heard people singing.

Behind him, across vast distances of space and time, from the place he had left, he thought he heard music too. But perhaps it was only an echo.

RELATED READINGS

Newbery Award Acceptance

by Lois Lowry

The Newbery Medal is the best-known U.S. award for writing in the field of children's literature. It is awarded to the author of the most distinguished contribution to literature for children published in the United States during the preceding year. The Giver *won the Newbery Medal for 1994. In her acceptance speech, author Lois Lowry explains how her own memories inspired ideas for her book.*

"How do you know where to start?" a child asked me once, in a schoolroom, where I'd been speaking to her class about the writing of books. I shrugged and smiled and told her that I just start wherever it feels right.

This evening it feels right to start by quoting a passage from *The Giver,* a scene set during the days in which the boy, Jonas, is beginning to look more deeply into the life that has been very superficial, beginning to see that his own past goes back further than he had ever known and has greater implications than he had ever suspected.

> . . . now he saw the familiar wide river beside the path differently. He saw all of the light and color and history it contained and carried in its slow-moving water; and he knew that there was an Elsewhere from which it came, and an Elsewhere to which it was going.

Every author is asked again and again the question we probably each have come to dread the most: HOW DID YOU GET THIS IDEA?

We give glib, quick answers because there are other hands raised, other kids in the audience waiting.

I'd like, tonight, to dispense with my usual flippancy and glibness and try to tell you the origins of this book. It is a little like Jonas looking into the river and realizing that it carries with it everything that has come from an Elsewhere. A spring, perhaps, at the beginning, bubbling up from the earth; then a trickle from a glacier; a mountain stream entering farther along; and each tributary bringing with it the collected bits and pieces from the past, from the distant, from the countless Elsewheres: all of it moving, mingled, in the current.

For me, the tributaries are memories, and I've selected only a few. I'll tell them to you chronologically. I have to go way back. I'm starting forty-six years ago.

In 1948, I am eleven years old. I have gone with my mother, sister, and brother to join my father, who has been in Tokyo for two years and will be there for several more.

We live there, in the center of that huge Japanese city, in a small American enclave with a very American name: Washington Heights. We live in an American style house, with American neighbors, and our little community has its own movie theater, which shows American movies; and a small church, a tiny library, and an elementary school; and in many ways it is an odd replica of a United States village.

(In later, adult years I was to ask my mother why we had lived there instead of taking advantage of the opportunity to live within the Japanese community and to learn and experience a different way of life. But she seemed surprised by my question. She said that we lived where we did because it was comfortable. It was familiar. It was safe.)

At eleven years old I am not a particularly adventurous child, nor am I a rebellious one. But I have always been *curious*.

I have a bicycle. Again and again—countless times —without my parents' knowledge, I ride my bicycle out the back gate of the fence that surrounds our comfortable, familiar, safe American community. I ride down a hill because I am curious and I enter, riding down that hill, an unfamiliar, slightly uncomfortable, perhaps even unsafe—though I never feel it to be—area of Tokyo that throbs with life.

It is a district called Shibuya. It is crowded with shops and people and theaters and street vendors and the day-to-day bustle of Japanese life.

I remember, still, after all these years, the smells: fish and fertilizer and charcoal; the sounds: music and shouting and the clatter of wooden shoes and wooden sticks and wooden wheels; and the colors: I remember the babies and toddlers dressed in bright pink and orange and red, most of all; but I remember, too, the dark blue uniforms of the schoolchildren: the strangers who are my own age.

I wander through Shibuya day after day during those years when I am eleven, twelve, and thirteen. I love the feel of it, the vigor and the garish brightness and the noise: all of such a contrast to my own life.

But I never talk to anyone. I am not frightened of the people, who are so different from me, but I am shy. I watch the children shouting and playing around a school, and they are children my age, and they watch me in return; but we never speak to one another.

One afternoon I am standing on a street corner when a woman near me reaches out, touches my hair, and says something. I back away, startled, because my knowledge of the language is poor and I misunderstand her words. I think she has said, "*Kirai-des'*" meaning that she dislikes me; and I am embarrassed, and confused, wondering what I have done wrong: how I have disgraced myself.

Then, after a moment, I realize my mistake. She has said, actually, "*Kirei-des'*." She has called me pretty. And I look for her, in the crowd, at least to smile, perhaps to say thank you if I can overcome my shyness enough to speak. But she is gone.

I remember this moment—this instant of communication gone awry—again and again over the years. Perhaps this is where the river starts.

In 1954 and 1955 I am a college freshman, living in a very small dormitory, actually a converted private home, with a group of perhaps fourteen other girls. We are very much alike. We wear the same sort of clothes: cashmere sweaters and plaid wool skirts, knee socks, and loafers. We all smoke Marlboro cigarettes and we knit—usually argyle socks for our boyfriends—and play bridge. Sometimes we study; and we get good grades because we are all the cream of the crop, the valedictorians and class presidents from our high schools all over the United States.

One of the girls in our dorm is not like the rest of us. She doesn't wear our uniform. She wears blue jeans instead of skirts, and she doesn't curl her hair or knit or play bridge. She doesn't date or go to fraternity parties and dances.

She's a smart girl, a good student, a pleasant enough person, but she is different, somehow alien, and that makes us uncomfortable. We react with a kind of mindless cruelty. We don't tease or torment her, but we do something worse: we ignore her. We pretend that she doesn't exist. In a small house of fourteen young women, we make one invisible.

Somehow, by shutting her out, we make ourselves feel comfortable. Familiar. Safe.

I think of her now and then as the years pass. Those thoughts—fleeting, but profoundly remorseful —enter the current of the river.

In the summer of 1979, I am sent by a magazine I am working for to an island off the coast of Maine to write an article about a painter who lives there alone. I spend a good deal of time with this man, and we talk a lot about color. It is clear to me that although I am a highly visual person—a person who sees and appreciates form and composition and color —this man's capacity for seeing color goes far beyond mine.

I photograph him while I am there, and I keep a copy of his photograph for myself because there is something about his face—his eyes—which haunts me.

Later I hear that he has become blind.

I think about him—his name is Carl Nelson—from time to time. His photograph hangs over my desk. I wonder what it was like for him to lose the colors about which he was so impassioned.

I wish, in a whimsical way, that he could have somehow magically given me the capacity to see the way he did.

A little bubble begins, a little spurt, which will trickle into the river.

In 1989 I go to a small village in Germany to attend the wedding of one of my sons. In an ancient church, he marries his Margret in a ceremony conducted in a language I do not speak and cannot understand.

But one section of the service is in English. A woman stands in the balcony of that old stone church and sings the words from the Bible: "Where you go, I will go. Your people will be my people."

How small the world has become, I think, looking around the church at the many people who sit there wishing happiness to my son and his new wife—wishing it in their own language as I am wishing it in mine. *We are all each other's people now,* I find myself thinking.

Can you feel that this memory, too, is a stream that is now entering the river?

Another fragment. My father, nearing 90, is in a nursing home. My brother and I have hung family pictures on the walls of his room. During a visit, he and I are talking about the people in the pictures. One is my sister, my parents' first child, who died young of cancer. My father smiles, looking at her picture. "That's your sister," he says happily. "That's Helen."

Then he comments, a little puzzled, but not at all sad, "I can't remember exactly what happened to her."

We can forget pain, I think. *And it is* comfortable *to do so.*

But I also wonder briefly: *is it* safe *to do that, to forget?*

That uncertainty pours itself into the river of thought which will become the book.

1991. I am in an auditorium somewhere. I have spoken at length about my book, *Number the Stars,* which has been honored with the 1990 Newbery Medal. A woman raises her hand. When the turn for her question comes, she sighs very loudly and says, "Why do we have to tell this Holocaust thing over and over? Is it really *necessary?*"

I answer her as well as I can—quoting, in fact, my German daughter-in-law, who has said to me, "No one knows better than we Germans that we must tell this again and again."

But I think about her question - and my answer - a great deal. Wouldn't it, I think, playing Devil's Advocate to myself, make for a more comfortable world to *forget* the Holocaust? And I remember once again how comfortable, familiar, and safe, my parents had sought to make my childhood by shielding me from Elsewhere. But I remember, too, that my response had been to open the gate again and again. My instinct had been a child's attempt to see for myself what lay beyond the wall.

The thinking becomes another tributary into the river of thought that will create *The Giver.*

Here's another memory. I am sitting in a booth with my daughter in a little Beacon Hill pub where she and I often have lunch together. The television is on in the background, behind the bar, as it always is. She and I are talking. Suddenly I gesture to her. I say, "Shhh" because I have heard a fragment of the news and I am startled, anxious, and want to hear the rest. Someone has walked into a fast-food place with an automatic weapon and randomly killed a number of people. My daughter stops talking and waits while I listen to the rest.

Then I relax. I say to her, in a relieved voice, "It's all right. It was in Oklahoma." (Or perhaps it was Alabama. Or Indiana.)

She stares at me in amazement that I have said such a hideous thing.

How *comfortable* I made myself feel for a moment, by reducing my own realm of caring to my own familiar neighborhood. How *safe* I deluded myself into feeling.

I think about that, and it becomes a torrent that enters the flow of a river turbulent by now, and clogged with memories and thoughts and ideas that begin to mesh and intertwine. The river begins to seek a place to spill over.

When Jonas meets The Giver for the first time, and tries to comprehend what lies before him, he says, in confusion, "I thought there was only us. I thought there was only now."

In beginning to write *The Giver*, I created, as I always do, in every book, a world that existed only in my imagination—the world of "only us, only now." I tried to make Jonas's world seem familiar, comfortable, and safe, and I tried to seduce the reader. I seduced myself along the way. It *did* feel good, that world. I got rid of all the things I fear and dislike: all the violence, prejudice, poverty, and injustice; and I even threw in good manners as a way of life because I liked the idea of it.

One child has pointed out, in a letter, that the people in Jonas's world didn't even have to do dishes.

It was very, very tempting to leave it at that.

But I've never been a writer of fairy tales. And if I've learned anything through that river of memories, it is that we can't live in a walled world, in an "only us, only now" world where we are all the same and feel safe. We would have to sacrifice too much. The richness of color and diversity would disappear. Feelings for other humans would no longer be necessary. Choices would be obsolete.

And besides, I had ridden my bike Elsewhere as a child, and liked it there, but had never been brave enough to tell anyone about it. So it was time.

A letter that I've kept for a very long time is from a child who has read my book called *Anastasia Krupnik*. Her letter—she's a little girl named Paula from Louisville, Kentucky—says:

> I really like the book you wrote about Anastasia and her family because it made me laugh every time I read it. I especially liked when it said she didn't want to have a baby brother in the house because she had to clean up after him every time and change his diaper when her mother and father aren't home and she doesn't like to give him a bath and watch him all the time and put him to sleep every night while her mother goes to work . . .

Here's the fascinating thing: *nothing that the child describes actually happens in the book.* The child—as we all do—has brought her own life to a book. She has found a place, a place in the pages of a book, that shares her own frustrations and feelings.

And the same thing is happening—as I hoped it would happen—with *The Giver.*

Those of you who hoped that I would stand here tonight and reveal the "true" ending, the "right" interpretation of the ending, will be disappointed. There isn't one. There's a right one for each of us, and it depends on our own beliefs, our own hopes.

Let me tell you a few endings which are the right endings for a few children out of the many who have written to me.

From a sixth grader: "I think that when they were traveling they were traveling in a circle. When they came to Elsewhere it was their old community, but they had accepted the memories and all the feelings that go along with it . . . "

From another: "Jonas was kind of like Jesus because he took the pain for everyone else in the community so they wouldn't have to suffer. And, at the very end of the book, when Jonas and Gabe reached the place that they knew as Elsewhere, you described Elsewhere as if it were Heaven."

And one more: "A lot of people I know would hate that ending, but not me. I loved it. Mainly because I got to make the book happy. I decided they made it. They made it to the past. I decided the past was our world, and the future was their world. It was parallel worlds."

Finally, from one seventh-grade boy: "I was really surprised that they just died at the end. That was a bummer. You could of made them stay alive, I thought."

Very few find it a bummer. Most of the young readers who have written to me have perceived the magic of the circular journey. The truth that we go out and come back, and that what we come back to is changed, and so are we. Perhaps I have been traveling in a circle, too. Things come together and become complete.

Here is what I've come back to:

The daughter who was with me and looked at me in horror the day I fell victim to thinking we were "only us, only now" (and that what happened in Oklahoma, or Alabama, or Indiana didn't matter) was the first person to read the manuscript of *The Giver.*

The college classmate who was "different" lives, last I heard, very happily in New Jersey with another woman who shares her life. I can only hope that she has forgiven those of us who were young in a more frightened and less enlightened time.

My son, and Margret, his German wife—the one who reminded me how important it is to tell our stories again and again, painful though they often are —now have a little girl who will be the receiver of all of their memories. Their daughter had crossed the

Atlantic three times before she was six months old. Presumably my granddaughter will never be fearful of Elsewhere.

Carl Nelson, the man who lost colors but not the memory of them, is the face on the cover of the book. He died in 1989 but left a vibrant legacy of paintings. One hangs now in my home.

And I am especially happy to stand here tonight on this platform with Allen Say because it truly brings my journey full circle. Allen was twelve years old when I was. He lived in Shibuya, that alien Elsewhere that I went to as a child on a bicycle. He was one of the Other, the Different, the dark-eyed children in blue school uniforms, and I was too timid then to do more than stand at the edge of their schoolyard, smile shyly, and wonder what their lives were like.

Now I can say to Allen what I wish I could have said then: "Watashi-no tomodachi des." Greetings, my friend.

I have been asked whether the Newbery Medal is, actually, an odd sort of burden in terms of the greater responsibility one feels. Whether one is paralyzed by it, fearful of being able to live up to the standards it represents.

For me the opposite has been true. I think the 1990 Newbery freed me to risk failure.

Other people took that risk with me, of course. One was my editor, Walter Lorraine, who has never to my knowledge been afraid to take a chance. Walter cares more about what a book has to say than he does about whether he can turn it into a stuffed animal or a calendar or a movie.

The Newbery Committee was gutsy, too. There would have been safer books. More comfortable books. More familiar books. They took a trip beyond the realm of sameness with this one, and I think they should be very proud of that.

And all of you, as well. Let me say something to those of you here who do such dangerous work.

The man that I named The Giver passed along to the boy knowledge, history, memories, color, pain, laughter, love, and truth. Every time you place a book in the hands of a child, you do the same thing.

It is very risky.

But each time a child opens a book, he pushes open the gate that separates him from Elsewhere. It gives him choices. It gives him freedom.

Those are magnificent, wonderfully *unsafe* things.

I have been greatly honored by you now, two times. It is impossible to express my gratitude for that. Perhaps the only way, really, is to return to Boston, to my office, to my desk, and to go back to work in hopes that whatever I do next will justify the faith in me that this medal represents.

There are other rivers flowing.

The Role of the Griot

by D'Jimo Kouyate

The griot is an important figure in traditional African societies. Compare and contrast the role of the griot from Senegal with the role of the Giver.

It is important that people understand the roles and the power that the griot (known as "jali" and prefixed before the given family name) has been endowed with since the beginning. One of the roles the griot in African society had before the Europeans came was maintaining a cultural and historical past with that of the present. He informed, even to this day, man and woman of the roles they must play in traditional African society. The griot was the oral historian and educator in any given society. The griot was well respected and was very close to kings—in fact, closer to the king than the king's own wife.

The griot served as the king's confidant and personal advisor. The griot would interpret things, such as different facts, for the king. It was also the responsibility of the griot to make sure that the people received all the information about their ancestors—what the father, the grandparents, and their lineages had done and how they had done it. What the griot gave to African society in oral history, cultural information, and ancestral wisdom and knowledge is the key with which all people of African descent can progress and maintain a high level of understanding of their true heritage.

All people of African descent—the Latin, the

Jamaican, the Haitian, the Brazilian, the Caribbean, and the African American—all must realize that, although they were not born in Africa, they are still African people and *all* of us have been through the experience of slavery. Most of us have lost our original language and traditions because of having been born outside of the African homeland. When you are away from your ancestral land and lack the necessary cultural information, you become "lost" by concept. The color of the skin remains the same but the concept, the knowledge of Africa, is gone. The traditional names and roles in society, everything that belonged to us by birthright, was taken away from most of us.

This is known as "the painful period." In order to get back what was ours, information and knowledge about African society and culture must be learned now. This the griot gives to all who need it. Our children need to have the facts about their ancestral homeland. This destiny will take a while, however. Everyone has a transition period. When a black person understands his or her African past, accepts being African, he is different from one who does not know these things. Those of us who know, know our value.

The reason I begin with this kind of conversation is that I want people to have the right idea about Africa and the role of the griot in the past and in today's time, so that everyone can understand the "capacity" and potential power that we still have today. This power must be used in a good way so that we can help one another. We are still a proud people and know the significant role we have and the part we must play in our humanity.

So the young man and woman, everybody who stays in the village, get a chance to listen, to live and learn about their culture and such things as I have been saying. In West African society there are various types of stories to communicate these principles. In the evening, after dinner, the stories that are usually told by the griot are called *tahlió* (tah-lee-OH), which means it is not the reality but an imagined event between humans and animals and some kind of spirit. These are the stories that are told for entertainment. A griot has special ways of telling these stories so that they are very entertaining, even though the griot's main intention is not to entertain but to teach the people to know themselves. When *tahlió* takes place, everybody participates. Know, too, that music is not always used and that the stringed harp-like instrument, the kora, for which griots are noted, is new in comparison to other African instruments.

We have to be all that we can be to get our art and all true information about the griot and our rich cultural folklore "out of the closet" in modern society. Most of us know all about the white man's education, his schools, history, and culture, but we lack the necessary information about our own.

I hope that someday we will have the young generation follow you and me and each of us who is working hard at keeping African culture and tradition alive. Yes, we need our stories; without stories in an oral tradition, there is no history, no reference. As the song says: *Sy-yáh Cáh*-pee-sah ma *loo* dee." Death is natural but I won't take humiliation; which means, if you don't know, you have to learn. Knowledge is learned. When one does not learn, that is humiliation.

Jeremiah's Song

by Walter Dean Myers

*What, if anything, can we learn from the
experiences of our ancestors? In the
following story, the narrator must decide
whether such memories are bridges to the
past or just a waste of time.*

I knowed my cousin Ellie was gonna be mad when
Macon Smith come around to the house. She didn't
have no use for Macon even when things was going
right, and when Grandpa Jeremiah was fixing to die
I just knowed she wasn't gonna be liking him
hanging around. Grandpa Jeremiah raised Ellie after
her folks died and they used to be real close. Then
she got to go on to college and when she come back
the first year she was different. She didn't want to
hear all them stories he used to tell her anymore.
Ellie said the stories wasn't true, and that's why she
didn't want to hear them.

I didn't know if they was true or not. Tell the truth
I didn't think much on it either way, but I liked to
hear them stories. Grandpa Jeremiah said they
wasn't stories anyway, they was songs.

"They the songs of my people," he used to say.

I didn't see how they was songs, not regular songs
anyway. Every little thing we did down in Curry
seemed to matter to Ellie that first summer she come
home from college. You couldn't do nothin' that was
gonna please her. She didn't even come to church
much. 'Course she come on Sunday or everybody
would have had a regular fit, but she didn't come on
Thursday nights and she didn't come on Saturday
even though she used to sing in the gospel choir.

"I guess they teachin' her somethin' worthwhile up there at Greensboro," Grandpa Jeremiah said to Sister Todd. "I sure don't see what it is, though."

"You ain't never had no book learning, Jeremiah," Sister Todd shot back. She wiped at where a trickle of sweat made a little path through the white dusting powder she put on her chest to keep cool. "Them old ways you got ain't got nothing for these young folks."

"I guess you right," Grandpa Jeremiah said.

He said it but I could see he didn't like it none. He was a big man with a big head and had most all his hair even if it was white. All that summer, instead of sitting on the porch telling stories like he used to when I was real little, he would sit out there by himself while Ellie stayed in the house and watched the television or read a book. Sometimes I would think about asking him to tell me one of them stories he used to tell but they was too scary now that I didn't have nobody to sleep with but myself. I asked Ellie to sleep with me but she wouldn't.

"You're nine years old," she said, sounding real proper. "You're old enough to sleep alone."

I *knew* that. I just wanted her to sleep with me because I liked sleeping with her. Before she went off to college she used to put cocoa butter on her arms and face and it would smell real nice. When she come back from college she put something else on, but that smelled nice too.

It was right after Ellie went back to school that Grandpa Jeremiah had him a stroke and Macon started coming around. I think his mama probably made him come at first, but you could see he liked it. Macon had always been around, sitting over near the stuck window at church or going on the blueberry truck when we went picking down at Mister

Gregory's place. For a long time he was just another kid, even though he was older'n me, but then, all of a sudden, he growed something fierce. I used to be up to his shoulder one time and then, before I could turn around good, I was only up to his shirt pocket. He changed too. When he used to just hang around with the other boys and play ball or shoot at birds he would laugh a lot. He didn't laugh so much anymore and I figured he was just about grown. When Grandpa got sick he used to come around and help out with things around the house that was too hard for me to do. I mean, I could have done all the chores, but it would just take me longer.

When the work for the day was finished and the sows fed, Grandpa would kind of ease into one of his stories and Macon, he would sit and listen to them and be real interested. I didn't mind listening to the stories when Grandpa told them to Macon because he would be telling them in the middle of the afternoon and they would be past my mind by the time I had to go to bed.

Macon had an old guitar he used to mess with, too. He wasn't too bad on it, and sometimes Grandpa would tell him to play us a tune. He could play something he called "the Delta Blues" real good, but when Sister Todd or somebody from the church come around he'd play "Precious Lord" or "Just a Closer Walk With Thee."

Grandpa Jeremiah had been feeling poorly from that stroke, and one of his legs got a little drag to it. Just about the time Ellie come from school the next summer he was real sick. He was breathing loud so you could hear it even in the next room and he would stay in bed a lot even when there was something that needed doing or fixing.

"I don't think he's going to make it much longer,"

Dr. Crawford said. "The only thing I can do is to give him something for the pain."

"Are you sure of your diagnosis?" Ellie asked. She was sitting around the table with Sister Todd, Deacon Turner, and his little skinny yellow wife.

Dr. Crawford looked at Ellie like he was surprised to hear her talking. "Yes, I'm sure," he said. "He had tests a few weeks ago and his condition was bad then."

"How much time he got?" Sister Todd asked.

"Maybe a week or two at best," Dr. Crawford said.

When he said that, Deacon Turner's wife started crying and goin' on and I give her a hard look but she just went on. I was the one who loved Grandpa Jeremiah the most and she didn't hardly even know him so I didn't see why she was crying.

Everybody started tiptoeing around the house after that. They would go in and ask Grandpa Jeremiah if he was comfortable and stuff like that or take him some food or a cold glass of lemonade.

Sister Todd come over and stayed with us. Mostly what she did is make supper and do a lot of praying, which was good because I figured that maybe God would do something to make Grandpa Jeremiah well. When she wasn't doing that she was piecing on a fancy quilt she was making for some white people in Wilmington.

Ellie, she went around asking everybody how they felt about Dr. Crawford and then she went into town and asked about the tests and things. Sister Jenkins asked her if she thought she knowed more than Dr. Crawford, and Ellie rolled her eyes at her, but Sister Jenkins was reading out her Bible and didn't make no notice of it.

Then Macon come over.

He had been away on what he called "a little piece of a job" and hadn't heard how bad off Grandpa Jeremiah was. When he come over he talked to Ellie and she told him what was going on and then he got him a soft drink from the refrigerator and sat out on the porch and before you know it he was crying.

You could look at his face and tell the difference between him sweating and the tears. The sweat was close against his skin and shiny and the tears come down fatter and more sparkly.

Macon sat on the porch, without saying a word, until the sun went down and the crickets started chirping and carrying on. Then he went in to where Grandpa Jeremiah was and stayed in there for a long time.

Sister Todd was saying that Grandpa Jeremiah needed his rest and Ellie went in to see what Macon was doing. Then she come out real mad.

"He got Grandpa telling those old stories again," Ellie said. "I told him Grandpa needed his rest and for him not to be staying all night."

He did leave soon, but bright and early the next morning Macon was back again. This time he brought his guitar with him and he went on in to Grandpa Jeremiah's room. I went in, too.

Grandpa Jeremiah's room smelled terrible. It was all closed up so no drafts could get on him and the whole room was smelled down with disinfect and medicine. Grandpa Jeremiah lay propped up on the bed and he was so gray he looked scary. His hair wasn't combed down and his head on the pillow with his white hair sticking out was enough to send me flying if Macon hadn't been there. He was skinny, too. He looked like his skin got loose on his bones, and when he lifted his arms, it hung down like he was just wearing it instead of it being a part of him.

Macon sat slant-shouldered with his guitar across his lap. He was messin' with the guitar, not making any music, but just going over the strings as Grandpa talked.

"Old Carrie went around out back to where they kept the pigs penned up and she felt a cold wind across her face. . . ." Grandpa Jeremiah was telling the story about how a old woman out-tricked the Devil and got her son back. I had heard the story before, and I knew it was pretty scary. "When she felt the cold breeze she didn't blink nary an eye, but looked straight ahead. . . ."

All the time Grandpa Jeremiah was talking I could see Macon fingering his guitar. I tried to imagine what it would be like if he was actually plucking the strings. I tried to fix my mind on that because I didn't like the way the story went with the old woman wrestling with the Devil.

We sat there for nearly all the afternoon until Ellie and Sister Todd come in and said that supper was ready. Me and Macon went out and ate some collard greens, ham hocks, and rice. Then Macon he went back in and listened to some more of Grandpa's stories until it was time for him to go home. I wasn't about to go in there and listen to no stories at night.

Dr. Crawford come around a few days later and said that Grandpa Jeremiah was doing a little better.

"You think the Good Lord gonna pull him through?" Sister Todd asked.

"I don't tell the Good Lord what He should or should not be doing," Dr. Crawford said, looking over at Sister Todd and at Ellie. "I just said that *my* patient seems to be doing okay for his condition."

"He been telling Macon all his stories," I said.

"Macon doesn't seem to understand that Grandpa Jeremiah needs his strength," Ellie said. "Now that he's improving, we don't want him to have a setback."

"No use in stopping him from telling his stories," Dr. Crawford said. "If it makes him feel good it's as good as any medicine I can give him."

I saw that this didn't set with Ellie, and when Dr. Crawford had left I asked her why.

"Dr. Crawford means well," she said, "but we have to get away from the kind of life that keeps us in the past."

She didn't say why we should be trying to get away from the stories and I really didn't care too much. All I knew was that when Macon was sitting in the room with Grandpa Jeremiah I wasn't nearly as scared as I used to be when it was just me and Ellie listening. I told that to Macon.

"You getting to be a big man, that's all," he said.

That was true. Me and Macon was getting to be good friends, too. I didn't even mind so much when he started being friends with Ellie later. It seemed kind of natural, almost like Macon was supposed to be there with us instead of just visiting.

Grandpa wasn't getting no better, but he wasn't getting no worse, either.

"You liking Macon now?" I asked Ellie when we got to the middle of July. She was dishing out a plate of smothered chops for him and I hadn't even heard him ask for anything to eat.

"Macon's funny," Ellie said, not answering my question. "He's in there listening to all of those old stories like he's really interested in them. It's almost as if he and Grandpa Jeremiah are talking about something more than the stories, a secret language."

I didn't think I was supposed to say anything about that to Macon, but once, when Ellie, Sister Todd, and Macon were out on the porch shelling butter beans after Grandpa got tired and was resting, I went into his room and told him what Ellie had said.

"She said that?" Grandpa Jeremiah's face was skinny and old looking but his eyes looked like a baby's, they was so bright.

"Right there in the kitchen is where she said it," I said. "And I don't know what it mean but I was wondering about it."

"I didn't think she had any feeling for them stories," Grandpa Jeremiah said. "If she think we talking secrets, maybe she don't."

"I think she getting a feeling for Macon," I said.

"That's okay, too," Grandpa Jeremiah said. "They both young."

"Yeah, but them stories you be telling, Grandpa, they about old people who lived a long time ago," I said.

"Well, those the folks you got to know about," Grandpa Jeremiah said. "You think on what those folks been through, and what they was feeling, and you add it up with what you been through and what you been feeling, then you got you something."

"What you got Grandpa?"

"You got you a bridge," Grandpa said. "And a meaning. Then when things get so hard you about to break, you can sneak across that bridge and see some folks who went before you and see how they didn't break. Some got bent and some got twisted and a few fell along the way, but they didn't break."

"Am I going to break, Grandpa?"

"You? As strong as you is?" Grandpa Jeremiah pushed himself up on his elbow and give me a look. "No way you going to break, boy. You gonna be strong as they come. One day you gonna tell all them stories I told you to your young'uns and they'll be as strong as you."

"Suppose I ain't got no stories, can I make some up?"

"Sure you can, boy. You make 'em up and twist 'em around. Don't make no mind. Long as you got 'em."

"Is that what Macon is doing?" I asked. "Making up stories to play on his guitar?"

"He'll do with 'em what he see fit, I suppose," Grandpa Jeremiah said. "Can't ask more than that from a man."

It rained the first three days of August. It wasn't a hard rain but it rained anyway. The mailman said it was good for the crops over East but I didn't care about that so I didn't pay him no mind. What I did mind was when it rain like that the field mice come in and get in things like the flour bin and I always got the blame for leaving it open.

When the rain stopped I was pretty glad. Macon come over and sat with Grandpa and had something to eat with us. Sister Todd come over, too.

"How Grandpa doing?" Sister Todd asked. "They been asking about him in the church."

"He's doing all right," Ellie said.

"He's kind of quiet today," Macon said. "He was just talking about how the hogs needed breeding."

"He must have run out of stories to tell," Sister Todd said. "He'll be repeating on himself like my father used to do. That's the way I *hear* old folks get."

Everybody laughed at that because Sister Todd was pretty old, too. Maybe we was all happy because the sun was out after so much rain. When Sister Todd went in to take Grandpa Jeremiah a plate of potato salad with no mayonnaise like he liked it, she told him about how people was asking for him and he told her to tell them he was doing okay and to remember him in their prayers.

Sister Todd came over the next afternoon, too, with some rhubarb pie with cheese on it, which is my favorite pie. When she took a piece into Grandpa Jeremiah's room she come right out again and told Ellie to go fetch the Bible.

It was a hot day when they had the funeral. Mostly everybody was there. The church was hot as anything, even though they had the window open. Some yellowjacks flew in and buzzed around Sister Todd's niece and then around Deacon Turner's wife and settled right on her hat and stayed there until we all stood and sang "Soon-a Will Be Done."

At the graveyard Macon played "Precious Lord" and I cried hard even though I told myself that I wasn't going to cry the way Ellie and Sister Todd was, but it was such a sad thing when we left and Grandpa Jeremiah was still out to the grave that I couldn't help it.

During the funeral and all, Macon kind of told everybody where to go and where to sit and which of the three cars to ride in. After it was over he come by the house and sat on the front porch and played on his guitar. Ellie was standing leaning against the rail and she was crying but it wasn't a hard crying. It was a soft crying, the kind that last inside of you for a long time.

Macon was playing a tune I hadn't heard before. I thought it might have been what he was working at when Grandpa Jeremiah was telling him those stories and I watched his fingers but I couldn't tell if it was or not. It wasn't nothing special, that tune Macon was playing, maybe halfway between them Delta blues he would do when Sister Todd wasn't around and something you would play at church. It was something different and something the same at the same time. I watched his fingers go over that guitar and figured I could learn that tune one day if I had a mind to.

The Pedestrian

by Ray Bradbury

Ray Bradbury is famous for his stories about life in the future for the common person. How does his vision of society compare to Lowry's futuristic world?

To enter out into that silence that was the city at eight o'clock of a misty evening in November, to put your feet upon that buckling concrete walk, to step over grassy seams and make your way, hands in pockets, through the silences, that was what Mr. Leonard Mead most dearly loved to do. He would stand upon the corner of an intersection and peer down long moonlit avenues of sidewalk in four directions, deciding which way to go, but it really made no difference; he was alone in this world of A.D. 2052, or as good as alone, and with a final decision made, a path selected, he would stride off, sending patterns of frosty air before him like the smoke of a cigar.

Sometimes he would walk for hours and miles and return only at midnight to his house. And on his way he would see the cottages and homes with their dark windows, and it was not unlike walking through a graveyard where only the faintest glimmers of firefly light appeared in flickers behind the windows. Sudden grey phantoms seemed to manifest upon inner room walls where a curtain was still undrawn against the night, or there were whisperings and murmurs where a window in a tomb-like building was still open.

Mr. Leonard Mead would pause, cock his head, listen, look, and march on, his feet making no noise on the lumpy walk. For long ago he had wisely changed to sneakers when strolling at night, because the dogs in intermittent squads would parallel his journey with barkings if he wore hard heels, and lights might click on and faces appear and an entire street be startled by the passing of a lone figure, himself, in the early November evening.

On this particular evening he began his journey in a westerly direction, toward the hidden sea. There was a good crystal frost in the air; it cut the nose and made the lungs blaze like a Christmas tree inside; you could feel the cold light going on and off, all the branches filled with invisible snow. He listened to the faint push of his soft shoes through autumn leaves with satisfaction, and whistled a cold quiet whistle between his teeth, occasionally picking up a leaf as he passed, examining its skeletal pattern in the infrequent lamplights as he went on, smelling its rusty smell.

"Hello, in there," he whispered to every house on every side as he moved. "What's up to-night on Channel 4, Channel 7, Channel 9? Where are the cowboys rushing, and do I see the United States Cavalry over the next hill to the rescue?"

The street was silent and long and empty, with only his shadow moving like the shadow of a hawk in mid-country. If he closed his eyes and stood very still, frozen, he could imagine himself upon the centre of a plain, a wintry, windless Arizona desert with no house in a thousand miles, and only dry river beds, the streets, for company.

"What is it now?" he asked the houses, noticing his wrist watch. "Eight-thirty p.m.? Time for a dozen assorted murders? A quiz? A revue? A comedian falling off the stage?"

Was that a murmur of laughter from within a

moon-white house? He hesitated, but went on when nothing more happened. He stumbled over a particularly uneven section of sidewalk. The cement was vanishing under flowers and grass. In ten years of walking by night or day, for thousands of miles, he had never met another person walking, not one in all that time.

He came to a cloverleaf intersection which stood silent where two main highways crossed the town. During the day it was a thunderous surge of cars, the gas stations open, a great insect rustling and a ceaseless jockeying for position as the scarab-beetles, a faint incense puttering from their exhausts, skimmed homeward to the far directions. But now these highways, too, were like streams in a dry season, all stone and bed and moon radiance.

He turned back on a side street, circling around toward his home. He was within a block of his destination when the lone car turned a corner quite suddenly and flashed a fierce white cone of light upon him. He stood entranced, not unlike a night moth, stunned by the illumination, and then drawn toward it.

A metallic voice called to him:

"Stand still. Stay where you are! Don't move!"

He halted.

"Put up your hands!"

"But—" he said.

"Your hands up! Or we'll shoot!"

The police, of course, but what a rare, incredible thing; in a city of three million, there was only *one* police car left, wasn't that correct? Ever since a year ago, 2052, the election year, the force had been cut down from three cars to one. Crime was ebbing; there was no need now for the police, save for this one lone car wandering and wandering the empty streets.

"Your name?" said the police car in a metallic whisper. He couldn't see the men in it for the bright light in his eyes.

"Leonard Mead," he said.

"Speak up!"

"Leonard Mead!"

"Business or profession?"

"I guess you'd call me a writer."

"No profession," said the police car, as if talking to itself. The light held him fixed, like a museum specimen, needle thrust through chest.

"You might say that," said Mr. Mead. He hadn't written in years. Magazines and books didn't sell any more. Everything went on in the tomb-like houses at night now, he thought, continuing his fancy. The tombs, ill-lit by television light, where the people sat like the dead, the grey or multicoloured lights touching their faces, but never really touching *them*.

"No profession," said the phonograph voice, hissing. "What are you doing out?"

"Walking," said Leonard Mead.

"Walking!"

"Just walking," he said simply, but his face felt cold.

"Walking, just walking, walking?"

"Yes, sir."

"Walking where? For what?"

"Walking for air. Walking to see."

"Your address!"

"Eleven South Saint James Street."

"And there is air *in* your house, you have an air *conditioner*, Mr. Mead?"

"Yes."

"And you have a viewing screen in your house to see with?"

"No."

"No?" There was a crackling quiet that in itself was an accusation.

"Are you married, Mr. Mead?"

"No."

"Not married," said the police voice behind the fiery beam. The moon was high and clear among the stars and the houses were grey and silent.

"Nobody wanted me," said Leonard Mead with a smile.

"Don't speak unless you're spoken to!"

Leonard Mead waited in the cold night.

"Just *walking,* Mr. Mead?"

"Yes."

"But you haven't explained for what purpose."

"I explained; for air, and to see, and just to walk."

"Have you done this often?"

"Every night for years."

The police car sat in the centre of the street with its radio throat faintly humming.

"Well, Mr. Mead," it said.

"Is that all?" he asked politely.

"Yes," said the voice. "Here." There was a sigh, a pop. The back door of the police car sprang wide. "Get in."

"Wait a minute, I haven't done anything!"

"Get in."

"I protest!"

"Mr. Mead."

He walked like a man suddenly drunk. As he passed the front window of the car he looked in. As he had expected, there was no one in the front seat, no one in the car at all.

"Get in."

He put his hand to the door and peered into the back seat, which was a little cell, a little black jail with bars. It smelled of riveted steel. It smelled of harsh antiseptic; it smelled too clean and hard and metallic. There was nothing soft there.

"Now if you had a wife to give you an alibi," said the iron voice. "But—"

"Where are you taking me?"

The car hesitated, or rather gave a faint whirring click, as if information, somewhere, was dripping card by punch-slotted card under electric eyes. "To the Psychiatric Centre for Research on Regressive Tendencies."

He got in. The door shut with a soft thud. The police car rolled through the night avenues, flashing its dim lights ahead.

They passed one house on one street a moment later, one house in an entire city of houses that were dark, but this one particular house had all of its electric lights brightly lit, every window a loud yellow illumination, square and warm in the cool darkness.

"That's *my* house," said Leonard Mead.

No one answered him.

The car moved down the empty river-bed streets and off away, leaving the empty streets with the empty sidewalks, and no sound and no motion all the rest of the chill November night.

The Forecast

by Dan Jaffe

*As a Giver, Jonas would experience a life
filled with the best and worst of human
experiences. The speaker in this poem tells
about life in a "safe" but restricted
environment. Which life would you
choose?*

Perhaps our age has driven us indoors.
We sprawl in the semi-darkness, dreaming
    sometimes
Of a vague world spinning in the wind.
But we have snapped our locks, pulled down
    our shades,
5 Taken all precautions. We shall not be dis-
    turbed.
If the earth shakes, it will be on a screen;
And if the prairie wind spills down our
    streets
And covers us with leaves, the weatherman
    will tell us.

Old Glory

by Bruce Coville

*To Jonas, the freedom to choose was
worth risking his life. In this story, two
characters also make decisions about the
cost of freedom.*

Donald Henderson   Ms. Barnan
Civic Responsibility Class   Sept. 15, 2041

ESSAY: The Day I Did My Duty
by
Donald B. Henderson

My great-grandfather was the craziest man I ever
met. Sometimes it was embarrassing even to have
him be part of the family.

For example: You should have seen how he acted
when Congress passed the S.O.S. law last June.

He actually *turned off* the holo set!

"Well that's the end of life as we know it," he said
as the image started to fade. Then he stared at the
floor and started to mutter.

"Oh, Arthur, don't be ridiculous," said my mother.

She switched the set back on and waited for the
newsgeek to reappear in the center of the room.

"Ridiculous?" yelped Gran-Da. "You want to see
ridiculous? I'll show you ridiculous!" He stood up
and pointed to the big flag that hangs over our holo
set. "That's ridiculous! Thirteen stripes, sixty-two
stars, and not a bit of meaning. After what they did
today, it's all gone."

"That's not so, Grampa," said my father quietly.
His voice was low and soft, the way it gets when he's

really angry. "Now sit down and be quiet."

That was a relief. After Gran-Da came to live with us, I was always afraid he was going to get us into trouble. So I felt better whenever Dad made him be quiet. Sometimes I wished Dad would just throw him out. I didn't really want him sleeping on the streets, like all the old men I walk past on the way to school. But I didn't want to make our Uncle angry either.

Later that night, when I was going to bed, Gran-Da called me into his room.

"How you doing?" he asked.

I shrugged. "I'm okay."

Gran-Da smiled. "Are you afraid of me?"

I wanted to say no. Only that would have been a lie. So I just nodded my head.

"Afraid I'll talk dangerous?"

I nodded again. I didn't know what I would do if my friends were ever around when he started talking like he does sometimes. I knew what I *should* do, of course. But I didn't know if I could do it. I mean, he *was* my great-grandfather, even if he was crazy and wicked.

He looked sad. "Are all the kids at your school like you?" he asked.

"What do you mean?"

"Scared little sheep, afraid to talk."

"I'm not afraid to talk," I said loudly. "I just don't talk nonsense, like . . ."

I broke off.

"Like me?" he asked, scratching at the little fringe of white hair that circled the back of his head. (I don't know why he never got his head fixed. All the other great-grandfathers I know have full heads of hair, whatever color they want. Not mine.)

I looked away from him. Suddenly I realized what was wrong with his room. "Where's your flag?" I asked.

"I took it down."

I must have looked pretty funny. At least, the look on my face made him snort.

"How could you?" I asked in a whisper.

"It was easy," he said. "I just pulled out the tabs at the corners, and then—"

"Gran-Da!"

"Donald!" he replied. "When the government passed S.O.S., they took away the last thing that flag stood for. I don't want to look at it anymore."

He paused and stared at the floor for a while. I looked at the door, wondering if he would say anything if I just left

Suddenly he looked up again. "Listen, Donald. I'm ninety years old. That's not that old, these days—I could probably last another thirty."

That was no news. It was one of the reasons my mother was so upset when he moved in. I felt sorry for her. Thirty years of Gran-Da was my idea of a real nightmare.

"The thing is," he continued, "I'm just a normal guy, not a hero. But sometimes there's something you have to do, no matter what it costs you."

I looked at him in horror. "You're not going to do anything crazy, are you?" I felt sick in my stomach. Didn't he understand he could get us *all* in trouble? If he wasn't careful, the Uncles might come and take us away. I glanced at the ceiling, half expecting it to open up so that a giant hand could reach down and snatch my great-grandfather then and there.

"Why are you telling me this?" I asked at last.

"Maybe I'm hoping that if I scare you enough it will make you start to think." He shrugged. "Or maybe I just want to see what you'll do."

"Can I go now?"

"Yeah," he said bitterly. "Go on. Get out of here."

I slipped out of his room and ran down the hall to my own room. I flopped onto my bed and lay there, staring up at my beautiful flag and trembling.

I thought about Gran-Da all that night. I thought about him in school the next morning, while we were saying the pledge, and the Lord's Prayer, and reciting the names of the presidents. I remembered what Gran-Da had said the first time he heard me recite the list—that there had been more presidents than we were naming, that some of them were being left out.

I wanted to talk to my teacher, but I was afraid.

The next morning was Saturday. When Gran-Da came to breakfast he had a red band tied around his head. He was wearing a vest with fringe on it, a blue shirt, and faded blue pants; he was carrying a lumpy plastic bag. He had a button on his vest that looked like an upside-down Y with an extra stick coming out of it.

"What's that?" I asked, pointing to the button.

"A peace symbol," he said. He dropped the bag to the floor and settled into his chair.

"Really, Arthur," said my mother. "Don't you think this is carrying things a little too far?"

"S.O.S. was carrying things too far," said Gran-Da.

My father sighed. "Look, Grampa, it's not really a problem. If you don't break the rules, S.O.S. won't have any effect on you."

I was amazed to hear him say that. Then I decided he must be trying to get Gran-Da to calm down. It didn't work. Gran-Da shook his head stubbornly, and suddenly I knew what he had in the bag.

My throat got thick with fear. I couldn't finish my breakfast.

After breakfast I followed Gran-Da out of the house. He was heading for the town square. I was pretty sure I knew what he was planning. My stomach was churning. What if the Uncles thought he had polluted our whole family?

I could only think of one way to save us. I slipped into a televid booth to call my Uncle. When I told him what was happening he looked stern and shocked.

"You won't hold this against the rest of us, will you?" I asked nervously.

He shook his head. "Of course not," he said. "You've done the right thing. We'll have to come and talk to all of you when this is over, of course. But I wouldn't worry about it much."

The screen went blank. I hurried back out to the street.

I felt embarrassed, and frightened. But I was also a little excited. Would the S.O.S. men really show up? My friends would think I was a real hero. I hurried toward the town square.

Gran-Da was already there. He had climbed onto the bandstand, of all places, and he was shouting about S.O.S.

People looked at him nervously. To my surprise, a few actually stopped to listen. I stood beneath a large tree, about a hundred feet away. I didn't want to get too close.

Suddenly Gran-Da reached into the bag and pulled out the flag he had taken off his wall the night before. Holding the upper edge, he rolled it over the side of the bandstand. A slight breeze made the stripes slide and shift.

I covered my face with my hands and wished the terrible scene would end.

Where were the S.O.S. men?

"Friends!" cried Gran-Da. "When I was a boy, this piece of cloth used to stand for something. Yes, it did. In fact, it stood for a whole lot of things. Ideas.

Like that a man should be free to say what he thinks, and worship where he wants, and get together with other folks if it pleases him."

More people were stopping to listen now. Someone started to boo.

"But that's all over," shouted Gran-Da. "Bit by bit, piece by piece, we've given away all the things this used to stand for. S.O.S. was the end of it. Now this poor old flag doesn't stand for anything at all.

"That being so, I think it's time I put it out of its misery."

I looked around. Where were the S.O.S. men? Why didn't they get here?

Now that people realized what Gran-Da was going to do, they started to back away. Some of them left. I could tell that others wanted to, wanted to get as far away from the terrible thing he was about to do as they possibly could. But they couldn't bring themselves to go. They wanted to see if he would really do it.

Gran-Da raised the flag and lit a match.

"Good-bye, Old Glory," he said sadly. "It was a good idea while it lasted."

He touched the corner of the flag with the match. Nothing happened, of course, since like all flags it was made of flameproof material. You can't burn a flag even if you try.

Gran-Da knew that. He wasn't stupid—just crazy. A crazy, dangerous person—the kind who could ruin the wonderful country we've built.

Suddenly I saw the S.O.S. men. They looked beautiful in their blue pants, white shirts, and red vests.

Gran-Da saw them too. I know he did.

So it's not like it's my fault, really. He had a chance. Everyone knows that even though the new law allows for instant executions, the Shoot On Sight men are supposed to give a guy a chance.

But Gran-Da didn't care. When his first match went out he lit another one. He held it to the corner of the fireproof flag and just stood there smiling at the three men.

So everyone could see that he was crazy.

The men lifted their laser rifles. The leader counted to three, and they fired in unison.

The light sliced right through the old man. He toppled over the edge of the bandstand. The flag curled around him as he fell. He was still holding it when he hit the ground.

My throat got thick. I could feel tears at the corners of my eyes. Crazy, I know. But he was my great-grandfather, after all. So I don't think it was too bad to feel a *little* sad about what had happened.

That doesn't mean I don't think I did the right thing by calling the S.O.S. guys. I mean, think about it. What would happen if other people started to think like Gran-Da—crazy things, like that everybody should be allowed to say whatever they wanted to?

What kind of a world would that be?

Drawing by Ronnie C., Grade One

by Ruth Lechlitner

*The members of Jonas's community did
not perceive the rainbow of colors around
them. But each of us perceives the world
uniquely. What can you learn from this
poem about seeing the world around you?*

For the sky, blue. But the six-year-
old searching his crayon-box, finds
no blue to match that sky
framed by the window—a see-through shine
5   over treetops, housetops. The wax colors
hold only dead light, not this water-flash
thinning to silver
at morning's far edge.
Gray won't do, either:
10   gray is for rain that you make with
dark slanting lines down-paper
                              Try orange!

—Draw a large corner circle for sun, egg-
    yolk solid,
with yellow strokes, leaping outward
15   like fire bloom—a brightness shouting
flower-shape wind-shape joy-shape!

The boy sighs, with leg-twisting bliss creating
    . . .

It is done. The stubby crayons
(all ten of them) are stuffed back
20 bumpily into their box.

from The Landscape of Memory

by Milton Meltzer

A good memory can be a blessing or a curse. In this excerpt, Meltzer discusses people whose memories are exceptional.

There are some people whose power of memory is far beyond the normal. President Franklin D. Roosevelt's campaign manager, James A. Farley, could remember the names of twenty thousand persons met while politicking about the country. Cyrus, the Persian king, could call out of memory the names of every officer in his army as he gave them orders. Themistocles, the Greek statesman, is said to have learned the names of all the citizens of Athens.

Fabulous stories about the memories of musicians are plentiful. Arturo Toscanini, the conductor, was sent a musical score by a hopeful young composer, who got no response. Seventeen years later the two men met at a dinner party. The composer said, "I don't suppose you'd remember that I once sent you a piece of mine in the hope you'd perform it." The conductor replied that he did recall it, then went over to the piano and played it through from memory, pointing out the weaknesses that made him decide not to conduct it. Or to cite the prodigious memory of other musicians: Hans von Bülow, the German conductor, while riding the train from Hamburg to Berlin, read the score of a new symphony he had never seen or heard before, and then conducted it that evening without the score.

Mozart could compose a whole symphony in his head and later write down the complete orchestration from memory. At eight, Felix Mendelssohn knew Beethoven's symphonies by heart.

For more examples we can go to preliterate societies. Here, too, can be found astonishing feats of memory. The poems of the *Iliad* and the *Odyssey,* before Homer wrote them down, were kept alive by word of mouth, stored in the memory of the ancient Greeks. Together the two Homeric poems total some twenty-seven thousand lines. In the mountains of Yugoslavia, about fifty years ago, visiting scholars recorded epic songs from the memory of the local people. Such a song was often several thousand lines long and would take hours to sing. Experienced singers knew at least thirty such songs; some claimed to know a hundred. These were not fixed and previously composed texts but followed basic themes and formulas, with the singer improvising the song anew each time he sang the oral poetry.

In the African country of Liberia, oral historians remember the history of whole clans and tribes. Some suggest that perhaps preliterate people have particularly good memories to make up for being unable to write things down. But the lack of something doesn't cause something else. Lack of wings doesn't make you faster on your feet. Rather, a particular culture nourishes particular abilities. Oral poets in a nonliterate society are raised on a specific concept of poetry. That concept of poetry changes when literacy develops, and so does the concept of memory.

The brilliant British mathematician Alexander Craig Aitken (1895–1967) had a legendary memory in many fields. He could muster a host of facts about numbers, mathematics, and mathematicians. A fine violinist, he could play many pieces by heart and identify a great deal of music when allowed to hear only snatches of it. He was able to quote at length from English literature and recite long passages of both Latin and English poetry. His recall of events he witnessed was so sharp and reliable that others drew upon his memory as though he were a record book. He was always precise about names, dates, places. In teaching, he could read just once the names of a new class of thirty-five students and never have to consult the list again. Give him a numbered line from a volume of Virgil's poetry and he could recite the words in that line—and, the converse, tell you the number of the line if you fed him the words in it.

Great chess players are often gifted with a powerful memory. Paul Charles Morphy, born in New Orleans in 1837, was a child prodigy at chess. He became world champion. He could play blindfold chess, which requires perfect recall of every new position throughout the game. He often played blindfold against several opponents at the same time, none of them blindfold. He could recall every move in every game of hundreds played in his career. About four hundred of his games are preserved in the records because, after the game ended, he was able to dictate from memory all the moves.

Chess masters have learned and store in their memory about fifty thousand patterns of positions on the board, according to the scientist Herbert A. Simon. But he adds that experts in any field probably have memorized some fifty thousand clusters of information in their specialty.

Ancient history records many feats of memory. Seneca the Elder, a Roman teacher, could repeat two thousand names in the order given him. A man named Simplicias could recite Virgil backwards. The ancients valued such mental gymnastics highly. The Greek dramatist Aeschylus called memory "the mother of all wisdom." And Cicero, the Roman statesman and orator, said, "Memory is the treasury and guardian of all things."

In the Washington, D.C., of today there is a restaurant that serves hundreds of people at lunch and at dinner. Each customer orders French gourmet food that must be prepared perfectly. The maitre d'hôtel can remember specific dinners ordered over the past forty years by his customers. On any morning he can recall the orders of every customer of the day before, as well as their specific table and place setting. The capital knows Jacques Scardella for his staggering ability to match face, place, and palate.

The New Yorker magazine's film critic, Pauline Kael, is noted for her recall of almost every detail in movies going back to her early childhood. When she sees revivals of old pictures, she always knows what's coming in the next scene.

There are scholarly Jews who have memorized the Talmud, a compilation of Jewish law and tradition, both in its worded message and in its exact appearance on the printed page. That extraordinary feat of memory has been described by the Reverend Dr. David Philipson. There are twenty large volumes to the Babylonian Talmud, containing thousands of pages. Every printed edition has exactly the same number of pages and the same words on each page. Dr. Philipson met a Hebrew scholar from Poland who knew the whole Talmud by heart. If you opened one volume of the Talmud, say, at page 10, and placed a pin on a word, say, the fourth word in line 8, and then asked the scholar what word was in this same spot on page 38 or page 50 or any other page, pressing the pin through till it reached the desired page, he would then say the word, and it was always correct.

It meant he had visualized in his memory the entire Talmud; it was as though the pages of the Talmud were photographed upon his brain. There is some evidence that at one period the Talmud was handed down solely by memory. Perhaps the feat of such Jews is the survival of a custom among early Jewish students in many communities of Eastern Europe.

How unique is such a memory? It is by no means as rare as one would guess, says the neurologist Ulric Neisser. He refers to frequent secondhand reports of people with astonishing memory for pictures, musical scores, chess positions, business transactions, dramatic scripts, or faces. Most often, he adds, you hear of a kind of visual memory that enables one to recall whole pages of a book that's been read. Many people report having had that ability in early life, but of losing it by the end of their teens.

Psychologists have come across quite a few people they call "calendar calculators." They can tell what day of the week corresponds to a given date in the past. One example was a minister named Dryden W. Phelps, who lived in the late nineteenth and early twentieth centuries. He could recall some particular thing that had happened on any day of the last sixty years of his life, and do it immediately upon request. For instance, if he were asked what happened on March 6, 1879, in a few moments he would state what day of the week that was—Monday or Thursday or whatever—then give the weather for that day and describe some particular thing that happened.

People with "photographic memory" are often

heard of. There are quite a few examples of the remarkable ability to store visual information in the memory. A woman who taught at Harvard and was a skilled artist had that ability. She could project an exact image of a picture or a scene on her mental screen. The image kept all the detailed surface and color of the original. The image would remain still, as though fixed on canvas, permitting her to examine its every aspect.

The power of her visual recall was not confined to pictures. Long after reading a poem in a foreign language, she could recall how the poem looked on the printed page and write it out rapidly from the bottom line to the top line, reading it off the screen of her mind's eye.

This visual recall is known as eidetic imagery. The word "eidetic" comes from the Greek *eidos*, meaning "form" or "that which is seen." It seems to be found more often in children than in adults. Perhaps 5 to 10 percent of children have it. Such children can remember whole scenes with great accuracy, though the capacity generally fades in the adult years—why, no one knows.

Actually, eidetic imagery can be more than photographic. Some people have that kind of recall by ear. They can hear a whole symphony in their mind, with the full range of instruments playing. And some may have a tactile eidetic image. With their touch recall they can feel the texture of a sable fur in all its richness.

But "there is such a thing as too good a memory," warns Frederick K. Goodwin, research chief of the National Institute of Mental Health. Certain fears, phobias, obsessions, can overpower the personality with memories that are terribly damaging. Perhaps the most famous case of harm done by a memory that never fails is the story of "S."

S was a Russian, Solomon V. Shereshevskii, a young newspaper reporter in Moscow. In the early 1920s his editor sent him for a psychological evaluation. Nothing seemed wrong with his personality and he did his job well. But his memory amazed his co-workers. When he covered a story, his mind retained everything he observed—from the important to the most trivial details, including names, phone numbers, addresses—and all this without taking notes.

At the clinic the reporter was examined by Aleksandr Luria, an eminent psychologist, intensely interested in memory. Given all kinds of memory tests, S never failed them. Luria studied S from the 1920s to the l950s, writing a classic book about the case called *The Mind of a Mnemonist*. (A mnemonist is one who has acquired skills helping one to remember something. The word comes from the Greek *mneme*, the goddess of memory.)

Luria found no limit to the capacity of S's memory or to the length of time he retained a memory. S could recall testing sessions he had taken thirty years before, repeating a series of random numbers or letters memorized on that much earlier date. S changed jobs from time to time, shifting from reporter to efficiency expert to financial analyst and finally to professional mnemonist, making a living by public exhibitions of his amazing ability.

Luria soon learned that S remembered far better than most, and he had a special way of doing it. How? British psychologist Ian L. M. Hunter describes the method:

> He used the classical mnemonist's technique of imagining richly vivid, concrete mental pictures,

which he arranged in a chain of pairs. If given a 25-word list he might take an imaginary walk along a street that has a vivid succession of landmarks. He would represent the first word by a distinctively imaged picture which he would "locate" on the first landmark, and so on. During a single, and not too rapid, presentation of the word list, he would progressively devise such a chain of images that was extremely rich in perception-like properties. This would result in accurate, durable memorization. Even years afterwards, he would be able to recapitulate the chain of images, and so recall the list of words in either forward or backward sequence.

Such a superhuman memory became not a blessing but a curse. S was deeply upset because he could not forget what he had memorized in his performances. To escape the burden, he tried writing down the material and then burning the paper, but that did not drop it out of his mind. When he was talking to a friend, any word exchanged might evoke a flood of irrelevant or trivial memories that poured off his tongue and made him sound almost crazy. These undesired memories tripped him up, so that he could never stick to a single line of conversation. He dragged after him an unbelievable load of useless information. The biggest problem of his life was that he could not forget.

The story of S makes us recall what psychologist William James once said: "If we remembered everything we should be as ill as if we remembered nothing."

Acknowledgments

(*continued from page ii*)

Dan Jaffee: "The Forecast" by Dan Jaffee. Copyright © 1964 by Dan Jaffee. By permission of the author.

General Media International, Inc.: "Drawing by Ronnie C., Grade One" by Ruth Lechlitner, from *Saturday Review*, July 15, 1967. Reprinted by permission of The Saturday Review © 1967, S. R. Publications, Ltd.

Penguin Books USA Inc.: "The Case of S," from *The Landscape of Memory* by Milton Meltzer. Copyright © 1987 by Milton Meltzer. Used by permission of Viking Penguin, a division of Penguin Books USA Inc.